INSPIRE / PLAN / DISCOVER / EXPERIENCE

BALI
AND LOMBOK

BALI
AND LOMBOK

CONTENTS

DISCOVER 6

EXPERIENCE 60

NEED TO KNOW 190

Left: Statue of Ganesha with a flower necklace and
ceremonial offering at Pura Petitenget temple near Seminyak
Previous page: Lagoon in the centre of Candidasa

DISCOVER

Sunrise over Mount Rinjani, Lombok

WELCOME TO
BALI AND
LOMBOK

Two neighbouring islands nestled in the Indonesian archipelago, blessed with natural wonders, rich in culture and history and with an astonishing heritage of arts and crafts, this double-destination offers something for everyone.

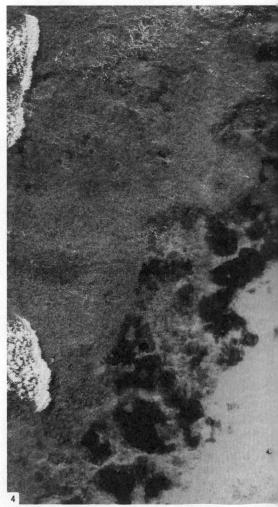

1 *Canang Sari* devotional flower offerings, Bali.

2 Mount Batur at sunrise, Bali.

3 Indonesian chicken satay dish.

4 Beach on Lombok with colourful umbrellas.

Bali and Lombok have a wealth of natural beauty to savour. Serrated coastlines frame hinterlands of lush, jungle-draped mountains and ancient volcanic calderas with shimmering crater lakes. Trek in the West Bali National Park, snorkel or dive the calm waters off Bali's north and east coast, surf the Bukit Peninsula or explore the beautiful nature of Nusa Penida island. In Lombok, relax on unspoiled, white-sand beaches, surf the southern breaks, escape to the Gili Islands, trek Mount Rinjani and visit the mountain villages of Sembalun and Senaru.

Although only 35 kilometres (22 miles) of sea separates these islands, the cultural distinctions between the predominately Hindu Bali and the largely Islamic Lombok are considerable, yet each beckons with its own fascinating traditions, festivals, music, dance, theatre and arts and crafts. Enjoy Bali's sophisticated international restaurants, shopping and nightlife in Seminyak, vegan cafés in Canggu and art museums and holistic healers in Ubud. For a quieter experience, head to the resorts of Senggigi and Kuta in Lombok. On both islands there are plentiful opportunities for bartering in markets or indulging in a relaxing massage at a spa retreat.

This guidebook breaks the islands down into easily navigable chapters, full of expert knowledge and insider tips. We've picked out themes and created detailed itineraries and colourful maps to help you plan the perfect trip. Whether you're on a flying visit or an extended adventure, this Eyewitness guide will ensure you experience the very best these two islands have to offer.

REASONS TO LOVE
BALI AND LOMBOK

From the tropical climate and the cuisine to the friendly people, rich cultures, artistic traditions, beaches and natural wonders, there is so much to love about these two beautiful islands.

1 GUNUNG KAWI ROYAL MONUMENTS

Bali's "Valley of the Kings" is one of the prettiest sites on the island. Descend through rice terraces to ancient shrines carved out of rock overlooking the Pakerisan River (p110).

NATURE AND WILDLIFE 2

From volcanoes, rainforests, lakes, river gorges and rice fields to cliffs and beaches, the islands' stunning natural landscapes are home to abundant flora and fauna.

3 GAMELAN MUSIC

Catch a performance of Bali's chiming gamelan percussion music, with its heavy bronze gongs, playful bamboo pipes, metallophones, drums, cymbals and flutes.

4 PURA LUHUR ULUWATU

High on the edge of a cliff above the ocean, this 11th-century temple glows with the radiance of the setting sun and will leave you with a powerful memory of spiritual Bali *(p66)*.

TREKKING MOUNT BATUR 5

Trekking to the summit of Gunung Batur volcano to see its crater lake and watch the sun rise behind the mighty Gunung Agung is a truly unforgettable experience *(p120)*.

SPAS 6

Spas in Bali and Lombok continue to sprout, grow and blossom like lotus flowers, offering traditional and modern body-soothing treatments *(p38)*.

SCUBA DIVING IN NUSA PENIDA 7

Attracting divers from all over the world, the clear waters off Nusa Penida teem with marine life, such as gorgeous corals, turtles, silver-tip sharks, manta rays and oceanic sunfish *(p88)*.

LOMBOK'S GILI ISLANDS 8

Did you know there are more than a dozen Gili Islands? Enjoy the famous Trawangan, Meno and Air *(p174)* or relish the seclusion of the "secret" Southwestern Gilis *(p189)*.

9 ART AND CULTURE IN UBUD

Whether dance, music, drama, paintings, carvings or hand-woven textiles, art in every form is at the heart of the highly valued Balinese culture whose epicentre is in Ubud *(p96)*.

10 TENGANAN BALI AGA VILLAGE

A lifestyle of ritual and ceremony is practised at this enchanting 700-year-old village. Expert artisans use centuries-old skills to create basketware and textiles *(p130)*.

JIMBARAN SEAFOOD FEAST 11

For seafood lovers, Jimbaran Bay is not to be missed. Lining the white-sand beach are dozens of simple stalls serving up the delicious catch of the day *(p82)*.

BEACHES OF BALI'S BUKIT PENINSULA 12

With secluded coves at the base of towering cliffs and white-gold sand pounded by world-famous surf breaks, the Bukit Peninsula has some of the island's most idyllic beaches.

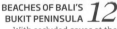

EXPLORE
BALI AND
LOMBOK

This guide divides Bali and Lombok into five colour-coded sightseeing areas, as shown on the map below. Find out more about each area on the following pages.

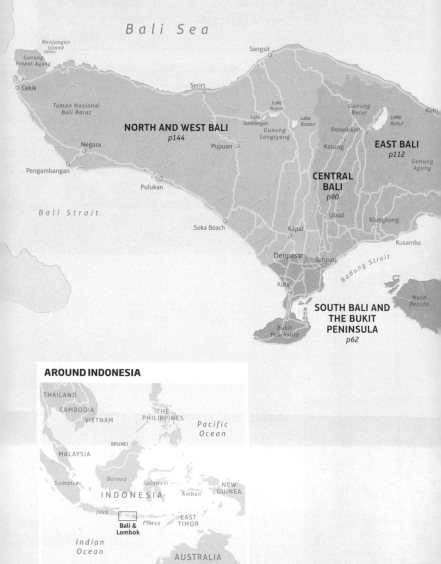

Bali Sea

Menjangan Island
Gunung Prapat Agung
Cekik

Sangsit

Serirt

Taman Nasional Bali Barat

NORTH AND WEST BALI
p144

Negara

Pengambangan

Pulukan

Bali Strait

Soka Beach

Lake Buyan
Lake Tamblingan
Gunung Sangiyang
Lake Braton

Gunung Batur
Penelokan
Katung

Lake Batur
Kubu

EAST BALI
p112

Gunung Agung

Pupuan

CENTRAL BALI
p90

Ubud

Kapal

Klungkung

Kusamba

Denpasar
Tohpati

Badung Strait

Kuta

Nusa Penida

SOUTH BALI AND THE BUKIT PENINSULA
p62

Bukit Peninsula

AROUND INDONESIA

THAILAND
CAMBODIA
VIETNAM
THE PHILIPPINES
Pacific Ocean
BRUNEI
MALAYSIA
Sumatra
Borneo
Sulawesi
NEW GUINEA
Ambon
INDONESIA
Java
Bali & Lombok
Flores
EAST TIMOR
Indian Ocean
AUSTRALIA

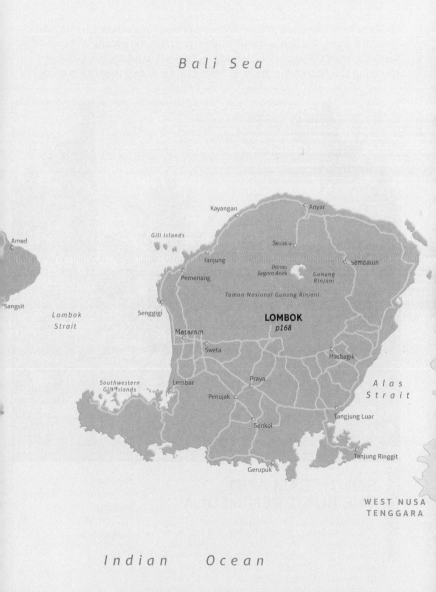

Bali Sea

Kayangan   Anyar

Gili Islands

Amed   Senaru

                    Tanjung   Sembalun
        Pemenang   Danau   Gunung
                            Segara Anak   Rinjani
Sangsit
        Lombok   Taman Nasional Gunung Rinjani
        Strait   Senggigi

                                    LOMBOK
                        Mataram   p168

                        Sweta
                                            Masbagik
                        Praya
        Southwestern   Alas
        Gili Islands   Lembar   Strait
                    Penujak

                                            Tangjung Luar
                    Senkol

                                            Tanjung Ringgit
                    Gerupuk

                                        WEST NUSA
                                        TENGGARA

        Indian   Ocean

                        0 kilometres   100   N

                        0 miles   100

GETTING TO KNOW
BALI AND LOMBOK

The islands of Bali and Lombok offer something for everyone, from exotic ancient history and rich cultures to abundant natural beauty and colourful festivals. With surfing, diving, trekking, cookery schools, yoga retreats, shopping and fine dining, there is a huge range of experiences to enjoy.

PAGE 62

SOUTH BALI AND THE BUKIT PENINSULA

White-sand beaches, secluded bays and a wide range of accommodation options, including lavish hotels and resorts, make South Bali a popular choice. The Bukit Peninsula, with its rugged coastline, clifftop views and watersports, is South Bali's highlight. At the south-western tip of the peninsula is Uluwatu, home to a stunning cliff-top temple and beaches famous for their surf breaks. Yet more beautiful nature can be enjoyed on the relatively undeveloped Nusa islands to the east.

Best for
Beaches; watersports; shopping

Home to
Pura Luhur Uluwatu

Experience
Seafood and beautiful sunset views over the sea

PAGE 90

CENTRAL BALI

Traditional arts and crafts communities, water temples, rice terraces, vertical river gorges and lush jungle are what characterize Central Bali. Numerous trails offer the opportunity to witness time-honoured methods of agriculture. The royal town of Ubud, Bali's artistic and cultural hub, is home to a treasure trove of art museums and galleries, a palace, market and monkey forest. Performances of traditional Balinese dance are staged here daily. Be inspired by the creativity all around, trek in beautiful forests or escape to a tranquil retreat for some meditation and yoga.

Best for
Art and culture; yoga

Home to
Ubud; Museum Puri Lukisan; Bali Bird Park

Experience
Mountain-biking; river-rafting; holistic therapies; watching a traditional dance performance

→

PAGE 112

EAST BALI

Peaceful East Bali offers a relaxing escape from the hustle and bustle of mainstream tourism, with its quiet beaches and calm, clear waters. This area is home to some of Bali's most significant royal palaces, water gardens and ancient villages. On a clear day, Gunung Agung, Bali's tallest and most sacred volcano, dominates the skyline. To the northeast, set within the crater of a vast and ancient caldera, is Bali's most-climbed volcano, Gunung Batur, overlooking Lake Batur in the spectacularly fertile Kintamani area.

Best for
Snorkelling; diving; rice-field and mountain trekking

Home to
Besakih Temple Complex; Gunung Batur; Pura Ulun Danu Batur; Klungkung; Taman Gili; Tenganan Bali Aga Village

Experience
Seeing the sunrise from the top of Mount Batur

PAGE 144

NORTH AND WEST BALI

With some of the island's most isolated and least-visited areas, this region is characterized by the unspoilt, rugged beauty and impenetrable highlands of the Taman Nasional Bali Barat (West Bali National Park). Further to the east is Bali's mountainous lake district, with spectacular waterfalls, rainforests and lakeside temples. Surfers will be attracted by the black-sand beaches and pummelling waves of the wild west, while divers and nature lovers are drawn to the dolphins and calm waters of the north coast, and the birds and wildlife in the national park.

Best for
Forest-trekking; horse-riding; bird-watching; wildlife-spotting

Home to
Taman Nasional Bali Barat; Singaraja; Pura Meduwe Karang; Pura Taman Ayun

Experience
Dolphin-watching at Lovina; the buffalo races at Negara

LOMBOK

Dominated by the mighty Mount Rinjani and bounded by divine beaches, picturesque bays, tiny paradisiacal islands, coral reefs and thrilling surf breaks, Lombok offers a myriad of natural attractions. It is perfect for the adventurous traveller in search of outdoor pursuits, such as surfing some of Indonesia's best waves, trekking the Rinjani National Park or seeking out hidden waterfalls. Divers and party-goers will love the northwest Gili Islands, while the less developed "secret" Southwestern Gili Islands offer a more tranquil getaway.

Best for
Trekking; snorkelling and diving; surfing

Home to
Taman Nasional Gunung Rinjani; Gili Islands

Experience
Bau Nyale Festival, held in February or March; traditional rural life

←

1 Rice terraces in the Sidemen Valley.

2 Preparing flower offerings for a temple festival in Tenganan Bali Aga Village.

3 Split entrance gate at Pura Agung Lempuyang Tara Penah.

4 Lotus lagoon in Candidasa.

These itineraries offer an array of ideas for exploring, leisure, historical insights, cultural pursuits and getting close to nature. Mix and match depending on your time available.

2 WEEKS

In Bali

Day 1

Starting at Sanur (p74), relax on the golden-sand beach or try a new watersport (ripcurlschoolofsurf.com/the-schools/sanur). Have lunch at a beachside eatery. A 20 minute stroll along the paved beach promenade brings you to the Le Mayeur Museum, the former 1930s home-studio of Belgian artist Adrien Le Mayeur. Dine on European-Asian fusion dishes in the cooling ocean breeze at Kayu Manis (p75).

Day 2

Leave Sanur early for the 66 km (41 mile) drive to Candidasa (p138) via the Sidemen Valley (p137). Stop for breakfast at Komune Resort (p104), overlooking the sparkling black sands of Keramas Beach. Continue to Klungkung and visit Taman Gili (p128) and the textile market (p125). Lunch at Warung Organic at Iseh (8 km/5 miles northeast of Sidemen), with a view of Mount Agung. Continue to Candidasa, enjoying more glorious views as you descend to the coast. Finish the day with dinner at Warung Lu Putu (www.dineincandidasa.com).

Day 3

Begin your day with a gentle hike to Bukit Asah, 2.5 miles/4 km from Candidasa. Enjoy the wonderful ocean views from the hilltop before continuing to the beautiful Virgin Beach (also known as Pasir Putih) (p139). Lunch at the beachside Virgin Café. After spending the afternoon lazing on the beach have dinner at Watergarden Café (www.watergardenhotel. com), with its menu of international dishes.

Day 4

Trek in the lush countryside around Candidasa with a local guide, such as Paleng (www.palengsbali.com/trekking.html). You will end at the fascinating Bali Aga village at Tenganan (p130). Return to Candidasa for lunch; visit the lotus lagoon, and then enjoy a blissful Balinese Healer treatment at Spa Alila Manggis (p39). Enjoy dinner in the romantic garden of Vincent's Restaurant (www.vincentsbali.com).

Day 5

Drive to Jasri (12 km/5 miles) for a tour of the delightful Sorga Organic Chocolate Factory (p140). Head north to Bali Asli (8.6 km/5.4 miles) for a gourmet lunch of organic Balinese cuisine and wonderful views (p143). Marvel at the architecture and stunning gardens of two lavish water palaces, Tirtagangga (p136) and Taman Ujung Water Palace (p139). The cheerful Warung Lesehan Mina Carik (Jalan Ahman Jani, Amlapura) is a great place for dinner.

Day 6

Drive 21 km (13 miles) to the hilltop temples of Pura Lempuyang (p140). If you don't fancy the climb up the 1,700 steps to the summit, stop at the first temple, Pura Agung Lempuyang Tara Penah, for an awe-inspiring vista of Mount Agung framed by the split gates. Continue to Amed (p141) through yet more eye-popping scenery. Spend the afternoon snorkelling around a Japanese shipwreck at Lipah Bay, an easy swim from the shore. Dine on local dishes at Warung Enak (p141).

→

Day 7

Wake up early to see the sunrise over Lombok and the little *jukung* fishing boats returning with the night's catch. Trek to the Five Holy Springs just outside Amed with a local guide. After lunch charter a traditional boat and captain for an exploration of the coastline. End the day with dinner at Sails Restaurant *(p141)*.

Day 8

Set out on a leisurely drive through starkly beautiful volcanic landscape along the coast to Lovina (88 km/55 miles) *(p166)*. Stop at the charming Cili Emas Oceanside Resort in Tejaula for lunch *(www.ciliemas. com)*. At the nearby village of Les, take a short walk through plantations of papaya and pineapple to Yeh Mempeh waterfall *(p167)*. Continue your drive, stopping to see the humorous relief carvings at Pura Dalem Jagaraga temple *(p167)*. Then drive through the wide streets of Singaraja *(p150)*, the former Dutch capital, for a glimpse of colonial grandeur. A 20-minute drive from here brings you to Lovina. Your hotel can arrange a morning dolphin-watching tour.

Day 9

Get up at the crack of dawn for your dolphin-watching excursion off Lovina in a traditional boat. Pods of dolphins come out every morning to play in the bay. Then head west to Pemuteran (45 km/28 miles), stopping off en route for a tour of Hatten Wines Vineyards at Sanggalangit *(p163)*. In the afternoon, snorkel or dive among the beautiful coral reefs at Pemuteran. Dine at the beachside Pondok Sari restaurant *(www.pondoksari.com)*.

Day 10

Set out early for Pura Puncak Manik (5km/3 miles), a beautiful small temple built around a sacred spring high up in the hills. You have to climb hundreds of steps, but when you reach the top, you will be rewarded with a marvellous view. Return to Pemuteran for lunch. Then drive to the Menjangan area (12 km/ 7.5 miles). Spend the afternoon relaxing at Pasir Putih Beach Club at the luxurious Menjangan Dynasty Resort *(mdr.pphotels. com)*, which has bathing pools fed by natural hot springs.

1 Gate in the Pura Taman Ayun royal temple, Mengwi.

2 Grapes in vineyards at Sanggalangit.

3 Dolphin-watching expedition off the coast of Lovina.

4 Enjoying sunset drinks at a beach bar on Seminyak Beach, just north of Kuta.

5 Bali Tower in the Menjangan Resort, overlooking the forest of the West Bali National Park and the landscape beyond.

Day 11

Snorkel or dive around Menjangan Island, famous for its flourishing marine life, lack of currents and crystal-clear waters. In the afternoon, head to the Menjangan Resort *(www.the menjangan.com)* to arrange a horse-riding excursion through Taman Nasional Bali Barat (West Bali National Park) *(p149)*. Later, climb the resort's Bali Tower for a sunset vista of monsoon forest, the East Java mountains, Menjangan Island and the Bali landscape, laid out like a map.

Day 12

Arrange for a national park guide to take you on an easy trek through West Bali National Park for some birdwatching and wildlife spotting. Enjoy lunch at Mimpi Resort Menjangan *(p163)*, followed by an afternoon relaxing in the healing waters of Mimpi's hot-spring bathing pools.

Day 13

Set out on the picturesque 136-km (85-mile) drive to Seminyak *(p79)*. Head east, stopping for a tour of Atlas South

Sea Pearl Farm at Penyabangan *(p163)*. Then turn inland at Sererit and drive south through the spectacular scenery of Pupuan for 65 km (41 miles) to Cempaka Belimbing Villas (www.cempakabelimbing.com) for lunch with a view of beautiful rice fields. Continue your journey, turning off the main road at Mengwi to visit the splendid garden-temple of Pura Taman Ayun *(p154)*, followed by another detour after 16 km (10 miles) to the dramatic sea temple of Tanah Lot *(p156)*. Continue to Seminyak. Dine at Mama San *(p78)*.

Day 14

Enjoy a gourmet breakfast at La Lucciola (Jalan Kayu Aya), overlooking the beach. Spend the morning visiting the markets near Seminyak Square. Lunch at Taco Beach Grill *(p78)*. In the afternoon, relax on Seminyak Beach and participate in the daily beach-bar sunset ritual, drinking a beer or a cocktail, while sitting on a bean-bag on the sand listening to live music. Have dinner on Jalan Petitenget, followed by a champagne cocktail at Red Carpet *(www.redcarpetchampagnebar.com)*.

→

1 Kuta Beach, lined with tropical-style resorts.

2 Traditional songket weaving at Sade village.

3 Pura Batu Bolong, on a rock jutting out to sea.

4 Horizon at Ashtari restaurant on a hilltop, Kuta.

10 DAYS

In Lombok and the Gili Islands

Day 1

From Lombok Airport drive south to Kuta (19 km/12 miles), and explore the Kuta Beach area *(p186)*. There is plenty of accommodation here. For a luxurious option, choose the beachfront Novotel Lombok *(www.novotellombok.com)*, 10 minutes' drive east of Kuta. Drive north (6 km/4 miles from Kuta) to Dusun Sade weaving village, whose shops stock a large range of woven fabrics. Head back south to Ashtari Lounge & Kitchen nearby (www.ashtarilombok.com) for a drink at sunset; nothing beats the view from here. If you're feeling active, join a sunset yoga class on the patio. Drive back to Kuta (4 km/2 miles) for dinner at Nugget's Corner *(p186)*, followed by cocktails in the laidback beachside Surfer's Bar (Jalan Raya Bunutan 1), which has live music on Fridays.

Day 2

Visit Putri Nyale Beach, 15 minutes' drive east of Kuta, a place of beauty and legend and the site of Lombok's famous Bau Nyale festival *(p187)*. At Seger Beach next door is a statue of the legendary Princess Mandalika. A seven-minute drive west will bring you to a roundabout at which you can turn back down to the coast to Mandalika Beach and the Novotel Lombok. Treat yourself to lunch amid the eccentric fairytale architecture of this stylish resort. Drive east to Tanjung Aan Beach (4 km/ 2.5 miles) *(p186)*, where there are reefs just offshore, perfect for snorkelling. Climb Merese Hill for gorgeous sunset views. For dinner, head to Bucu Restaurant and Bar *(p186)* for great Indonesian food.

Day 3

Drive to Mawun Beach (10 km/6 miles west of Kuta) *(p187)*. Stop for a swim and, if you'd like to try your hand at surfing, continue another 9 km (5 miles) west to Selong Belanak Beach *(p188)*, where the gentle waves are ideal for beginner surfers. Have lunch at the delightful Laut Biru Café *(sempiakvillas.com/laut-biru-bar-restaurant)*. Spend the afternoon lazing on the beach, rent a surfboard or charter a boat from the local fishermen for a fishing excursion. Be sure to be back in time to watch the buffaloes being herded along the water's edge at sunset. Kampung Café *(Jalan Selong Belanak)* is a good place for dinner, with its menu of delicious Indonesian and Western dishes.

Day 4

Head 40 km (25 miles) north to the intriguing traditional pottery village of Banyumelek *(p189)*. Tour the galleries to watch artisans at work, then continue 13 km (8 miles) north to Mataram*(p178)*. Stop for lunch here and visit Sekarbela village if you're interested in purchasing some fine-quality pearls. In the afternoon drive 18 km (11 miles) north to Senggigi *(p180)*. Pass the Hindu temple of Pura Batu Bolong, which juts out to sea straddling an archway in the rock. Explore Senggigi's beachfront, lined with cafés and restaurants. Enjoy a fine dinner at Square Restaurant *(p180)*, followed by a drink at one of the bars lining the beach.

$\rightarrow$

Day 5

Continue north to Bangsal, which is the departure point for the Gili Islands (p174). Take a public ferry to the island nearest to the mainland, Gili Air, explore the island on foot or by bicycle and enjoy lunch at one of the numerous cafés on the beach. Spend the afternoon snorkelling – there's a good chance you'll see a turtle. If you're a diver, don't miss the opportunity to see rare mandarinfish in the harbour at sunset, otherwise head to the west side of the island to watch the sunset to see Bali's Mount Agung silhouetted against a red sky. Have dinner lounging on comfy bean bags overlooking the ocean at Mowie's Bar (Jalan Gili Air).

Day 6

Wake up early to see the sunrise over Lombok's Mount Rinjani. Take a hopper boat to Gili Meno, the smallest and least-developed of the three northwestern Gili islands. Snorkel at Blue Coral Point off the northeast coast, which has a beautiful coral reef, or search for hawksbill or green turtles off the northwestern part of the island.

Jump on a hopper boat to the third and largest island, Gili Trawangan. Spend the afternoon either at a spa or, if you're feeling energetic, go on a guided horse ride around the island with Stud Stables. Dine beside the beach.

Day 7

Take the ferry back to Bangsal on the mainland for your 60-km (37-mile) journey to Senaru, gateway to Taman Nasional Gunung Rinjani national park (p173). Head northeast along the rollercoaster road hugging the dramatic coastline all the way from Senggigi to Anyar, where it drops inland to Bayan. Winding around the palm-fringed bays of Karang, Mangsit, Malimbu, Teluk Kodek, Nippah and Teluk, the road will treat you to fine views of the Gili Islands. At Bayan, thought to be the birthplace of the island's Wetu Telu religion (p179), stop outside Lombok's oldest mosque, a striking tiered building, constructed of bamboo and thatch atop a circular stone platform (p182). Check in to your accommodation at Senaru Rinjani Mountain Lodge (www.rinjanilodge.com),

1. Tiu Kelep Waterfall near Senaru.

2. Typical street on Gili Trawangan.

3. Lounging on beanbags at Mowie's Bar on Gili Air.

4. Sun setting behind Mount Agung, as seen from Gili Air.

5. Spa on Gili Trawangan.

6. Snorkelling off Gili Meno.

with its breathtaking views of the mountain. Grab a bite to eat in the restaurant there. In the afternoon, take a tour with one of the local women guides of the traditional Sasak village of Dusun Senaru and its gardens of fruits and spices. This is the oldest traditional village in Lombok, a living museum of grass-roofed, woven-bamboo houses. After dinner, sit on the open-air terrace of the restaurant or your room, and relish the sounds of nature.

Day 8

Wake up early to see the sunrise over Mount Rinjani. With a local guide, descend a well-trodden flight of steps through the tropical forest to Sindang Gila, a roaring 40-m (130-ft) tiered waterfall. Continue your walk alongside an old irrigation canal to the dazzling Tiu Kelep waterfall (p183). Take a dip in the pool beneath the falls and swim behind the main cascade; according to local legend you will emerge one year younger. Move back downstream and soak in the river's jacuzzi-like pools. In the afternoon drive to Sembalun (p182), which takes approximately two hours through awe-inspiring scenery on winding mountain roads. Check into a homestay for an authentic experience and home-cooked Sasak mountain cuisine. Unsullied by streetlights, the night sky over Sembalun is truly magnificent.

Day 9

Spend a day hiking with an official guide in the Taman Nasional Gunung Rinjani national park (p173). Not everyone comes here to climb the volcano: other trekking options include the nine-hour Sembalun Wildflowers Walk to see the stunning wildflowers at the Propok outlook.

Day 10

Depart Sembalun for the three-hour drive back to the airport. Stop en route at Sukarara weaving village, just 12 km (8 miles) from the airport. Here you can buy traditional songket textiles and watch the weavers at work.

←

1 Tegallalang rice terraces.

2 Monkeys and statuary in the Sacred Monkey Forest.

3 Traditional dance at Puri Saren.

4 Craftsman at work in an art studio.

5 DAYS
In Ubud

Day 1

Start with a walk through the Sacred Monkey Forest (p98). Remember to hold on to your hat and sunglasses! Then stroll up Jalan Hanoman (p99), stopping at the charming F.R.E.A.K coffee shop. Turn right at the top and you'll find Ubud market, with great handicrafts. Head west along the main road to the footpath at Abangan Bungalows, and take a 20-minute walk through the lovely rice fields to Sari Organic (Jalan Subak Sok Waya) for lunch. After lunch, explore the shops and arrange for a car and driver to take you to Petulu village (3 km/1.8 miles) for sunset (p108). Arrive by 5:30pm and watch thousands of herons and egrets roosting in the treetops. Return to Ubud for a traditional dance show at 7pm in the courtyard at the royal palace, Puri Saren (p96), and then dine at a traditional *warung* in the town centre.

Day 2

Yoga lovers should take the opportunity to salute the sun with a yoga session (www.theyogabarn.com). You'll need your own transport, or a car and driver, for the rest of the day for visiting Goa Gajah cave and temple (p106) before continuing on to lunch with a view at Kafe Kawi (inside the entrance of Pura Gunung Kawi) and an exploration of the temples at Tampaksiring (13 km/8 miles) (p110). In the evening, check out Laughing Buddha Bar in central Ubud (laughingbuddhabali.com) for live music.

Day 3

Visit Neka Art Museum (p98) for a a superb introduction to Balinese art. Walk 500 m (546 yards) to Indus Restaurant (www.casa luna bali.com/indus-restaurant) for lunch with a view across the valley. Afterwards, head to Jungle Fish Pool Club, in a stunning setting overhanging a river gorge, 4.5 km (3 miles) from Indus (www.chapung.com/eat and drink). Spend the afternoon relaxing by the pool. In the evening, chill out in the XL Shisha Lounge (Jalan Monkey Forest 129) with a shisha pipe and live music.

Day 4

Hire a car and tour-guide driver (we recommend www.putubalitourguide.com) and head to Kintamani to explore the lava fields at Mount Batur (p120). Lunch on the rim of the caldera with spectacular volcano and lake views. Visit Pura Ulun Danu Batur temple (p122) and drive back to Ubud via Tegallalang (p108), where there are stunning rice terraces. Stop for a drink at Kampung Cafe (p109), and shop for handicrafts from a multitude of workshop outlets. Spend your evening at Betelnut (Jalan Raya Ubud), where you can enjoy delicious Asian cuisine and perhaps a movie night, a talk, a dance performance or live music

Day 5

Visit Puri Lukisan art museum, followed by some of the art shops and contemporary galleries in Ubud centre. Have lunch at the legendary Murni's Warung (p98). In the afternoon, be eased into a state of total relaxation at Maya Ubud Spa (p39) – book in advance. Treat yourself to dinner at Hujan Locale (www.hujanlocale.com), followed by cocktails and live music at No Mas Bar (www.nomasubud.com).

→

① Hindu ceremony at Ulun Danu Bratan temple.

② Huge trees in the tropical jungle near Lake Tamblingan.

③ Balinese cocoa beans – some of the best in the world.

④ Munduk waterfall, a short walk from Munduk village.

3 DAYS
In Bali's Lake District

Day 1

Morning Begin at Mengwi at the Pod organic chocolate factory *(www.bali choklat.com)* for a tour and a tasting of the delicious products. Then drive to Baturiti, visit the traditional produce market and make a photo-stop looking east towards Mount Batur and Mount Agung. The small lakeside market town of Bedugul *(p166)* is heralded by a corn and cabbage statue. Turn left here onto Jalan Kebun Raya and stop for lunch at Eat Drink Love Café & Art Shop.

Afternoon Wander through the cool, shaded Bali Botanic Garden, with over 2,000 species of plants *(p166)*. Thrill-seekers will love to fly from tree to tree through suspended bridges, nets and Tarzan swings at the adjacent Bali Treetop Adventure Park. Allow two and a half hours here.

Evening Head back to Bedugul to Warung Recreasi near Lake Bratan *(www.warung rekreasi bedugul.com)*, a good option for both accommodation and dinner.

Day 2

Morning Golfers can enjoy an early-morning round at the spectacular Handara Golf Course *(www.handaragolfresort.com)*, the only golf course in the world that sits inside the crater of an extinct volcano. Others may enjoy browsing Bukit Mungsu market *(opposite Warung Recreasi)*, which has handicrafts and souvenirs, plus fruit and spices. Be sure to visit the mystical Ulun Danu Bratan Temple *(p166)* and have a taste of the locally grown strawberries at Strawberry Stop beside the lake (Jalan

Raya). Continue northwest along the main road. At the top of the hill, turn left towards Munduk village *(p165)*. This scenic route follows the rim of the ancient caldera and overlooks the northern shores of the twin lakes of Buyan and Tamblingan. Stop at Wanagiri Hidden Hills & Bali Swing, where viewing points invite you to pose for enviable Instagram photos. Continue to Munduk to the The View Restaurant *(Jalan Raya Kayu Putih)* for glorious views of the valley and a lunch of Indonesian delights.

Afternoon Enjoy a gentle trek through clove and coffee plantations to splash at three of the famous waterfalls: Munduk, Melanting and Laangan Melanting. The round trip takes about two hours.

Evening Stay overnight at Munduk, where accommodation is plentiful.

Day 3

Morning Head to the southwest side of Lake Tamblingan *(p165)*, where local guides will row you across the tranquil waters in a traditional canoe. Visit Pura Tahun and other hidden temples and trek through the tropical forest. Lunch at Ngiring Ngewedang *(www.ngiring ngewedang.com)* and relish the jaw-dropping vista.

Afternoon Walk 2.5 km (1.6 miles) to the tiny village of Munduk Tamblingan to see the Pura Dalem Gubug lakeside temple, with its tall meru on a small promontory. A path then leads through open pasture back to the village of Gubug. Spend the rest of the day relaxing and strolling through more of the enchanting countryside at your leisure.

Bali's Rice Fields

Bali is renowned for the beauty of its sculpted rice terraces. Estimated to cover 20 percent of Bali's land mass, these vibrant-green, layered plantings unfold like giant stairways descending from the mountains to the sea. The magnificence of these gorgeous hand-carved landscapes can fill entire memory cards with remarkable photographs.

←

Lush, terraced rice fields, with Mount Agung in the background

BALI AND LOMBOK'S
NATURAL WONDERS

Bali and Lombok are full of natural beauty. Volcanoes climb heavenwards into the clouds, deep and narrow river gorges, rugged saddles, plummeting waterfalls and primeval calderas etch and gouge the islands' landscapes, while mountain lakes shed life-giving water onto fertile plains.

Volcanic Peaks

Hiking up Lombok's Mount Rinjani is one of the most exhilarating experiences in Indonesia. A four-hour trek ascending 850 m (2,800 ft) above the village of Sembalun will reward you with a magnificent view of Propok – a dramatic flat valley and fertile green plain surrounded by mountains and tropical forest.

↑ The small, active volcano and lake inside the caldera of Mount Rinjani

Dizzying Cliffs and Coral Reefs

Soaring limestone sea cliffs typify Bali's Bukit Peninsula and the island of Nusa Penida. Seaweed farms layer the shallows like patchwork quilts, and ribbons of luminous turquoise water highlight coral reefs and an aquatic world reminiscent of a living kaleidoscope. Here, the powerful swells of the Indian Ocean create some of the world's most thrilling and sought-after surf breaks. There is a beautiful variety of coral in the waters around the Gili Islands off Lombok, which teem with pipe fish, lionfish, moray eels, turtles and much more.

←

Cliff in the shape of a Tyrannosaurus Rex at Kelingking Beach, Nusa Penida; sea turtle *(inset)*

Did You Know?

Bird-watchers can see well over 200 of Indonesia's bird species in Bali and Lombok.

Waterfalls

Sometimes the most spectacular natural wonders are the ones that are hardest to reach. Getting to Sekumpul Waterfall in Buleleng Regency in North Bali involves a three-hour hike past durian, rambutan and coffee plantations, complete with dirt tracks, crossings over streams and climbing about one hundred steps. The beautiful 80-m-(262-ft-) high waterfall is actually a cluster of six to seven narrow cascades that form the centrepiece of a lush-green bamboo-forested valley. These cascades are fed by two upland streams, and are the most accessible of a collection of falls within the area.

↑ The stunning Sekumpul Waterfall in North Bali, surrounded by greenery

33

◁ Balinese Cuisine
Considered to be one of the world's most complex cuisines, Balinese food is an elaborate blend of fresh ingredients, intricate flavours and aromatic spices, prepared with great attention to detail. There are no artificial flavourings, additives or colourings.

Indonesian Spices ▷
Indonesian cuisine is distinguished by the many freshly ground and blended spices that enliven and add depth to the dishes. Typical spices include ginger, turmeric, galangal, coriander, lemongrass and chillies, enhanced with shallots, garlic, candlenuts, pandan leaves and tamarind. The proper combination is regarded as an art in Indonesia, and delicate adjustments are made until the exact balance of flavours is achieved.

BALI AND LOMBOK FOR
FOOD LOVERS

The endless dining possibilities in Bali, and to a lesser extent in Lombok, cater to every taste, from *kaki-lima* (street-food) carts and tiny street-side eateries known as *warung* or *rumah makan* ("eating house") to seafood restaurants, vegan cafés and gourmet fine dining.

◁ Delicious Mangosteen
With a flavour said to be reminiscent of a fine peach, muscatel grapes and something indescribable which no other fruit has, it's not surprising that the mangosteen is held to be the most delectable of all Indonesia's tropical fruits. It is comprised of a deep-purple shell housing several segments of soft, juicy, pure-white pulp. The number of segments inside matches the number of petals found on the bottom of the shell.

◁ Seminyak, Bali's Foodie Capital

Bali has emerged as a major culinary destination in the 21st century. With the highest concentration of independent eateries on the island, Seminyak is its foodie capital. An abundance of uber-cool cafés and hip restaurants serve sensational cuisine from all around the world. The fine-dining experiences are enhanced by designer decor and celebrity chefs. Bon appétit!

Did You Know?

Food colourings are obtained from plants such as red hibiscus flowers and green pandan leaves.

◁ Jajan Pasar

Traditional Indonesian snacks and cakes, *jajan pasar* are steamed rather than baked, and therefore very different in texture, taste and appearance from Western cakes or pastries. Many of these moist, colourful delicacies are made with rice flour, coconut milk and palm sugar. Other ingredients might include cassava, tapioca, sago flour, eggs or mashed sweet potato. Typical flavourings are vanilla, durian and chocolate, while fillings often comprise beans, cheese and banana, or meat and carrots.

GET COOKING

The best way to find out more about the local cuisine is to sign up for a stimulating, hands-on cooking class in which you will learn how to prepare the basic *bumbu* spice mix, before going on to cook a complete feast that you can later savour at leisure. Classes are available in Bali and Lombok, and typically run for a full morning, followed by the chance to sample the fruits of your labour at lunch-time. Recommended cooking schools are Bumbu Bali in Tanjung Benoa and Gili Cooking Classes on Gili Air.

△ Fiery Lombok

For a destination with a name that loosely translates as "chilli", it's not surprising that Lombok's cuisine is highly regarded. You'll find a profusion of exotic tastes, textures and aromas, with more than a few spicy surprises. If you prefer fine dining to street eats, you can savour authentic Sasak flavours alongside familiar global fare, from Italian to Indian, in the main areas of Kuta, Senggigi and the Gili Islands.

Treetop Adventures

Hop from tree to tree like a squirrel at the fun Bali Treetop Adventure Park within the Bali Botanic Garden (p166). Circuits are tailored to suit all fitness levels and ages, from age 4 upwards. Suspended bridges, winches, ropes, nets and flying-fox ziplines let visitors explore the forest from well above the ground (www.bali treetop.com).

→

Tying onto a zip line at Bali Treetop Adventure Park

BALI AND LOMBOK FOR
FAMILIES

Bali is a paradise for kids, with plentiful activities for all the family. The island offers everything from adventure sports to theme parks, and most of the attractions are child-friendly. Lombok, meanwhile, is a natural wonderland, perfect for more adventurous families with older children.

Snorkelling and Swimming

Many of Lombok's pristine white-sand beaches are perfect for swimming and snorkelling, with clear turquoise water. Mawun Beach (p187) and the eastern side of Tanjung Aan Beach (p186) have sheltered bays. After swimming at Senggigi Beach be sure to watch the spectacular crimson sunset against a dramatic backdrop of the mighty Gunung Agung.

Snorkelling among corals in the clear waters off Lombok ↑

Turtle Release

The green and hawksbill turtles that inhabit Indonesia's coastal waters are considered endangered due to harvesting for meat, eggs and shells. Additionally, their existence is threatened by the loss of nesting grounds and water pollution. Turtle conservation initiatives in Bali retrieve the eggs and ensure they are incubated in a secured environment. The hatchlings are then cared for in a holding tank until they are strong enough to swim in the ocean. The heart-warming experience of releasing baby turtles, organized by the Bali Sea Turtle Society in Kuta between April and October, is especially popular with children, teaching them about conservation from an early age *(www.baliseaturtle.org)*.

←

Baby sea turtles being released; Hawksbill turtle hatchlings in a holding tank *(inset)*

📷 PICTURE PERFECT
Exotic Birds

At Bali Bird Park, pose for photos next to cockatoos, parrots, macaws, pelicans, hornbills or any number of other species of colourful bird *(p94)* – a photographer's heaven.

Get Wet at Waterbom

Voted the best of its kind in Asia, Bali's Waterbom Park is a fabulous theme park for a family day out, with rides, slides and leisure attractions to suit kids and adults of all ages. Waterslides include the Constrictor - a staggering 250 m (820 ft) in length - the Python, the Boomerang, the Pipeline and Climax, where you can reach speeds of up to 43 mph (70 kmph) *(www.waterbom-bali.com)*.

→

Floating down a stream at the fun Waterbom Park

The Bali Spa Experience

For a true escape, stay at one of Bali's exclusive spa retreats. Utilizing natural products and local village remedies is the universal concept of these establishments. In addition to traditional Balinese massage, treatments may include Ayurvedics, hot stone massage, Thai massage and barefoot Shiatsu. Energy treatment may include Watsu, in which the participant floats effortlessly while receiving gentle, water-assisted massage and stretches; chakra balancing sessions; craniosacral therapy; Reiki; and Chi Nei Tsang massage. Activities may include yoga, martial arts and meditation.

→ Chakra balancing in an infinity pool at a spa retreat

BALI AND LOMBOK FOR
WELLNESS

Ease fatigue, stimulate the senses and awaken the spirit at one of the many spas in Bali and Lombok. As well as luxury spa retreats, many hotels and beauty salons offer traditional and modern body-soothing treatments to enhance your overall wellbeing.

Healing Boreh

Boreh is a centuries-old remedy, traditionally used by Balinese villagers to relieve muscular aches and pains and boost circulation after long days of toiling in the rice fields. Warm, potent spices such as powdered sandalwood, cloves, cinnamon, coriander, turmeric and nutmeg are blended with rice powder into a fragrant paste and applied to the body as a warming, healing masque. Balinese Boreh is one of the most luxurious spa treatments available - wonderful not only for its relaxing and curative properties but also for exfoliating and softening the skin.

→ Traditional Indonesian spices used in Balinese spa treatments

TOP
3
SPA RETREATS

Spa Alila, Manggis
🅦alilahotels.com/
manggis/spa-alila
In a forest and
overlooking the sea,
this spa has two *bales*
for relaxing treatments.

Maya Ubud Spa
🅦maya resorts.
com/ubud/spa-
and-wellness
This large retreat has
luxury rooms and villas
and captures the spirit
of a Balinese village.

Prana Spa, Seminyak
🅦pranaspabali.com
Indulge in the rituals of
ancient kings and queens
at this exotic spa.

↑ A Balinese open-
  sided thatch *bale* for
  massage treatments

MANDI LULUR

Indonesia's famous
Mandi Lulur skin care
treatment originated
in the royal palaces of
Central Java. The ritual
begins with a body
massage, followed by
a skin exfoliation
utilizing a fragrant
paste blended from
sandalwood, turmeric,
ground nuts, rice,
herbs, jasmine flowers
and other exotic
ingredients. The
relaxing indulgence is
then completed with a
yogurt body mask.

↑ A relaxing head massage,
  improving blood flow for
  healthier skin

Massage

If it's massage you're after, check out Jari Menari (the name
means "Dancing Fingers"), which has branches in Seminyak
and Nusa Dua. Winner of multiple awards, it has highly trained,
all-male practitioners who focus on rhythm, flow and long
connective strokes, with strong, firm, consistent pressure.
The semi-open-air massage rooms are elegant and full of
natural light, each bordering a koi fish pond. If you're interested
in learning how to administer a massage, you can join one of
Jari Menari's regular day-long Learn Massage Workshops
(*www.jarimenari.com*).

Bali's Virgin Beach

Located near Candidasa, Virgin Beach, or Pasir Putih, meaning "white sands", is fringed by a coconut grove and flanked by green headlands and a sheer cliff *(p139)*. This idyllic stretch of sand is easily accessed by car. A more romantic approach to it, however, is by sea in a traditional *jukung* fishing boat *(www.palengsbali.com)*.

←

Virgin Beach, where you can rent sun loungers and umbrellas

BALI AND LOMBOK FOR
BEACH LOVERS

While Lombok is famous for its beaches of fine white sand, especially in the west and the south of the island, extending to a pink-sand beach in the southeast, Bali's coastline has a shifting palette of colours, ranging from white and gold through shades of brown, silver and grey to glittering black.

PICTURE PERFECT
Kelingking Beach

Indonesian for "little finger", Kelingking is Nusa Penida's most Instagrammed beach – a secluded golden-sand haven surrounded by turquoise waters at the bottom of a lofty cliff *(p33)*. Getting to the beach involves a hike down a 400-m (1,310-ft) perilously steep, narrow cliff-side track, so most people are content to photograph it from the cliff top.

Lombok's Southern Shores

Some of Lombok's most spectacular coastal scenery can be found on the southern shores of the island around Kuta, which presents a very different picture from its celebrated namesake in Bali. Here, windswept white- and golden-sand bays are separated by headlands and rocky outcrops. The glorious crescent-shaped beaches of Kuta and Tanjung Aan are famous for their surf breaks but when the tide is out, the bays turn into shallow pools of turquoise water *(p186)*.

→

The tropical paradise of Kuta Beach, Lombok, with clear turquoise water

Dream Beach, with its
white sand and blue sea,
Nusa Lembongan ↑

Dream Beach, Nusa Lembongan

On the island of Nusa Lembongan *(p89)* off the south coast
of Bali, Dream Beach is a gorgeous, secluded half-moon of
powdery white sand backed by mangroves. A restaurant,
beach club and hut-style accommodation can be found on the
cliff above this pandanus-fringed bay. Be sure to visit the nearby
Devil's Tear – a rocky outcrop and cove, where you'll see dramatic
waves crashing at full power
to create water plumes
and high-pressure
spouts; just don't
be tempted to
get too close
to the edge.

> HIDDEN GEM
> ### Pink Beach
>
> The spectacular Pantai
> Tangsi, or Pink Beach, in
> Southeast Lombok is
> untouched by mass
> tourism. Its colour comes
> from fragments of red
> coral washed up on the
> beach, which, when
> mixed with the sand,
> give it a pink hue.

Bukit Peninsula

Bali's Bukit Peninsula *(pp82–6)*
is home to some of the island's
most idyllic beaches. Many of
these beauty spots are at the
base of towering cliffs and
involve walking down steep
steps to reach them. Hang
around surfers in Bali and you
will hear mention of Uluwatu,
Padang Padang, Impossibles,
Bingin, Dreamland, Balangan,
Nyang Nyang and Green
Bowl – world-class surf
beaches named after waves
that break on shallow reefs
creating long tubes.

↑ Beach at Uluwatu, a world-famous
surfing spot on the Bukit Peninsula;
surfer at Padang Padang *(inset)*

▽ Art Markets

Bali is well known for its busy art markets. Most present a rambling scene of small kiosks within a semi-open-air complex. Others, such as the huge Kumbasari Art Market in Denpasar *(p70)*, are housed in a dedicated building. Crowded alleyways are crammed with vendors, buyers, artworks and handicrafts stretching in all directions. Haggling is essential and highly entertaining, with a lot of flamboyant gestures.

BALI AND LOMBOK'S
ARTS AND CRAFTS

The arts of Bali and Lombok are inseparable from the cultural and religious life of the communities; whether performing arts, painting or handicrafts, art in every form is the pinnacle of the local, highly esteemed culture. Individual villages in Bali and Lombok support specific crafts and art forms.

△ The Art of Batik

An ancient Indonesian art form, Batik designs are created by covering part of a fabric with wax and then dyeing it. The dye doesn't penetrate the wax, which is then melted away, before being reapplied to leave behind intricate multicoloured patterns. Motifs drawn with a wax-filled pen are called *batik tulis*. The wax can also be applied with a copper stamp, known as a *cap*.

INTERNATIONAL DEMAND

The rich artistic traditions of Bali have led to the evolution of a vibrant handicraft industry, in which pieces are created to be sold in local art shops and markets, as well as for export worldwide, providing business opportunities for many locals. Souvenirs and art objects range from trinkets, clothing, kites, woodcarvings and paintings to rare collectors' items.

▽ Art of Stone

Every kind of stone sculpture is produced on Bali, and styles vary from village to village, with many intricate designs for places of worship. Interestingly, there is little difference between the iconography decorating temples and that of private homes. Gateways represent the dividing line between the inner and outer worlds and, as such, are the recipients of some of the most fantastic carvings. Bali's main centre of stone carving is the village of Batubulan (p102).

△ Woodcarving

In Bali's woodcarving villages such as Mas (p105) and Tegallalang (p108), you will hear the gentle hammering and sanding of the woodcarvers as they sit cross-legged, surrounded by piles of woodchips. Using small tools and highly sharpened instruments, the master carver lightly taps, chips, chisels and picks away to create effigies, masks and ornaments.

▷ Pottery

Pottery is the main product of several villages in Lombok. Water decanters, decorated plates and saucers, vases, huge water containers and lamps are all created by hand. The pots crafted in Banyumulek (p189) are simple in design and devoid of embellishments; Masbagik specializes in distinctive geometric patterns and Penujak (p185) produces pots decorated with animal motifs.

◁ Natural Materials

A wide range of handicrafts, both practical and decorative, are made from natural fibres and materials, such as pandanus, rattan, banana leaves, bamboo, roots and grasses, bone, coconut shell and buffalo horn. Natural ornamentation is used to embellish these objects. You will even find boxes and model ships made entirely from cloves.

Splash Out

Bali's Tanjung Benoa *(p82)* has operators offering everything from wakeboarding, jet-skiing, parasailing and kayaking to banana boat rides and flying fish – an inflatable rubber boat that is pulled by a speedboat and flies up in the air. For all of these adventure watersports in Lombok, head to Senggigi *(p180)* or the Gili Islands *(p174)*.

←

Tandem parasailing, one of the popular watersports at Tanjung Benoa, Bali

BALI AND LOMBOK FOR
ADVENTURERS

The seas off Bali and Lombok provide plenty of opportunity for surfing, sailing, diving and all manner of other watersports. Inland, you can climb volcanoes, raft rivers, go canyoning through deep river gorges or try your hand at paragliding off cliff tops.

Go Canyoning

Bali and Lombok's vast river systems flow through deep canyon gorges. Canyoning, led by ICO Pro qualified instructors, involves following a river downstream while negotiating boulders, waterfalls and natural slides by means of trekking, caving, scrambling, climbing, abseiling, jumping, sliding and swimming. Established canyoning routes are near Bedugul and Kintamani in Bali and near Gumantar Village in North Lombok. The easiest trip takes about 1.5 hours and the more advanced routes can take 3-4 hours to complete, with waterfall abseils of about 50 m (164 ft) *(www.adventureandspirit.com; canyoninglombok.com)*.

→

Bali's stunning, rugged Beji Guwang Hidden Canyon, Sukawati

📷 PICTURE PERFECT
Jet of Energy

The magnificent jet of pure-white energy of the Tiu Kelep waterfall near Senaru in Lombok makes for a fantastic photo. You can swim in the pool below it *(p183)*.

Climb Mount Rinjani

If the idea of jumping out of your comfort zone and pushing yourself physically and mentally appeals, then you should challenge yourself to climb Lombok's eerily beautiful Mount Rinjani (p172). The three-day and two-night trek is a true bucket-list experience where you can swim in the crater lake next to the active, smoking cone of Rinjani's Gunung Baru and sleep in a tent teetering on the side of a crater rim (www.climbmtrinjani.com).

$\rightarrow$

Camping site on the ascent to the summit of Mount Rinjani, Lombok

Soar Like an Eagle

The best place for paragliding is Bali's Timbis Beach. Soar like an eagle along the shores of the Indian Ocean beside the picturesque cliffs. Every year, from May through to October, the southerly trade winds blow in off the Indian Ocean and allow for a 12-km (7.5-mile) flight above the sparkling sea (www.baliparagliding.com).

$\leftarrow$

Paragliding above the Indian Ocean off Timbis Beach on the Bukit Peninsula, South Bali

Raft Rivers

Enjoy the excitement of rafting on Bali's Ayung and Telaga Waja rivers against a backdrop of jungle, gorges, waterfalls and rice terraces. Professionally trained guides will give you instruction and work with you to safely navigate the raft through torrents, twists, tight turns and inclined rapids. If you like it particularly wild, go during the rainy season (Oct–Apr) (www.raftingbali.net).

$\rightarrow$

Whitewater rafting through the Ayung River Gorge in Ubud, Bali, a thrilling adventure

Canang Sari

Offerings to the gods are an integral part of day-to-day life for the Balinese, and can be seen everywhere in many different forms. When you walk down the street in Bali, you will most certainly notice the tiny, woven palm-frond trays that have been placed on the pavements and at the base of steps. These offerings, known as *canang sari*, are presented twice a day, with devotion, in front of homes and businesses, as well as at temples and shrines, on statues and even at crossroads, where they are believed to ward off accidents.

$\longrightarrow$

Palm-frond trays containing typical *canang sari* offerings

BALI AND LOMBOK'S
LOCAL CULTURE

There are many places to immerse yourself in Bali and Lombok's unique cultures. Sample local delicacies at night markets, visit museums, watch shows of dance performances and ritual music, witness Balinese Hindu and Lombok Sasak religious ceremonies and visit traditional villages.

Sasak man playing a Gendang Beleq drum in a village in Lombok ↑

Gendang Beleq

The distinctive music of Lombok, Gendang Beleq forms an important part of the island's culture. At most major events and ceremonies you will see a band of colourfully dressed musicians, playing, dancing and marching with their drums and other instruments.

 GREAT VIEW
Rice Terraces

Jatiluwih village *(p160)*, with its spellbinding vista of rolling rice terraces, is a UNESCO World Heritage Site for its preservation of traditional Balinese farming techniques.

INSIDER TIP
Where to See Dance Shows

Dance performances geared for tourists last 90 minutes. These are not inferior to sacred performances; in fact, some of the islands' best dancers and musicians perform for tourists. Many large hotels have regular evening dinner shows. Various forms of dance and drama can be seen at the annual Bali Arts Festival too (p52).

Dance Performances

The roots of Balinese dance are trance ritual and the Javanese theatrical forms known as *wayang*, where performers wear colourful masks and headdresses. Kecak dance is based on a trance formerly used in times of epidemic. Performances take place at religious ceremonies. In Lombok, the dances of the Sasak are ritual performances, often involving men in competition or combat.

←

A Balinese dancer in traditional make-up and costume

Rice Field Irrigation

Because of the island's long dry season, irrigation is critical to Balinese wet-rice agriculture. This is achieved through ancient aquatic engineering, managed by the farmers through village cooperatives known as *subak*. Water is diverted from rivers and streams and channelled through an elaborate system of canals, tunnels and aqueducts to the top of terraced rice fields. It then flows by gravity from field to field.

↑ Rice fields in Bali, watered by an irrigation system dating to the 11th century

The Lofty Stone Coconut Shell Temple

High on the slopes of Gunung Batukaru is Pura Luhur Batukaru *(p160)*, the "Lofty Stone Coconut Shell Temple", which venerates the deities of mountains and lakes, and was the ancestral temple for the royal family of Tabanan, whose descendants still maintain the shrines today. It is well worth visiting this mystical and deeply spiritual place, and pausing for a while to contemplate or meditate.

→

Pavilions in Pura Luhur Batukaru, located on the slopes of Gunung Batukaru

BALI'S
BEAUTIFUL TEMPLES

The temple or Pura is the focus of the spiritual activity of every community in Bali, a transient abode for the gods to occupy whenever they are invited. Open and unroofed for easy access between the worlds, the gates and walls serve only to keep impure and evil influences away.

Pura Kehen

A little off the main tourist path, but well worth a visit, is Pura Kehen *(p136)*, the state temple of the Bangli kingdom and the second largest in Bali. It is also one of the island's most beautiful and impressive temples, set on a wooded hillside in terraces lined with religious statues.

→

Pura Kehen temple, the former royal temple of the Bangli kingdom

📷 PICTURE PERFECT
Island Temple

Pura Tanah Lot *(p156)* is one of the most photographed sights in Bali. In the late afternoon, you can see a splendid profile of the temple silhouetted against the setting sun.

Pura Dalem Jagaraga

The lavishly decorated Pura Dalem Jagaraga near Singaraja *(p167)* is famous for its flamboyant stone carvings. The elaborate sculptured panels portray life during Dutch colonial times, including a Dutch steamer sending out a smoky SOS signal while being attacked by a sea monster, armed bandits holding up two smug Europeans riding in a vintage Ford car and World War II bi-planes engaged in an aerial battle, with some plunging into the sea.

← Detail of a stone carving on the Pura Dalem Jagaraga

Singaraja *(p167)*

FULL MOON BLESSINGS

The full moon, or Purnama, is considered to be a very auspicious day in Bali – an ideal time for healing, guidance and performing good deeds. On this sacred day, the gods are honoured with offerings of food, fruit and flowers. The Balinese Hindus believe that at every full moon the gods will descend to the earth to bestow their blessings, thereby initiating temple ceremonies and self-purification rituals performed using holy water, incense smoke, petals and rice grains.

Temple Processions

Any visitor who spends more than a few days in Bali is likely to see some kind of fascinating temple festival or colourful procession, an important and integral element of daily life on the island. In these processions, women carry stunningly crafted *gebogan* – mountain-shaped offerings of fruit on their heads. A lavish festival that commemorates the founding of a temple is called an Odalan.

↑ Devotees carrying elaborate, colourful offerings in a temple procession in Ubud

Gunung Batukaru

The extinct volcano of Batukaru (or Batukau) in Bali's Tabanan Regency is the island's second-highest peak *(p160)*. Located in an area that boasts the greatest biological diversity in Bali, its high alpine slopes are filled with mountain streams, ferns, wild flowers, creepers and orchids, as well as the rare black leaf-eating monkey, small forest deer, butterflies, flying lizards, the *landak* (porcupine) and the *lubak* (mongoose). Local guides lead visitors on anything from gentle hikes to challenging treks to the 2,276-m (7,500-ft) summit.

→

Gunung Batukaru, the source of irrigation water for the surrounding rice, coffee and fruit fields

BALI AND LOMBOK'S
SPECTACULAR VOLCANOES

Bali and Lombok sit on the volcanic "ring of fire" that stretches from Sumatra to the Banda Sea. The resplendent summits of Gunung Agung and Gunung Rinjani dominate the landscapes of these two neighbouring islands.

Gunung Seraya

At an elevation of 1,090 m (3,500 ft), Gunung Seraya towers over Bali's most easterly coast. For a gentle hike, start at Bangle village on the eastern slope, in the company of a guide, and trek to Toye Masem – the Five Holy Springs. The source of each spring is guarded by a shrine and is purported to spout a different taste. The ambitious can aim for the summit, which challenges even the most experienced hikers – at the top you will be rewarded with a breathtaking vista.

←

Gunung Seraya and Gunung Lempuyang seen against a backdrop of rice terraces

PICTURE PERFECT
Volcano and Rice Fields

On a clear day at sunrise, the central and eastern volcanoes of the mighty Gunung Batukaru make a dramatic appearance across the fields to create a backdrop to a perfect photo.

← Trekking Gunung Batukaru at sunrise, worth the challenge for the views at its summit

Gunung Catur

Standing on the eastern side of Lake Bratan (p166) is the extinct Gunung Catur. At 1,861 m (6,100 ft), it is the fourth-highest mountain in Bali, with dense forest covering its slopes. The hike to the top takes about three hours amid gorgeous scenery. You will see long-tailed monkeys and pass various shrines and former Dutch colonial weekend retreats. The view from the summit, looking down over Lake Tamblingan, is spectacular. On the rim of the caldera is the Pura Pucak Mangu temple, built around 1830.

HIDDEN GEM
Crater Lake

The caldera of Lombok's Gunung Rinjani (p172) is partially filled by a dazzling, mystifyingly blue, crescent-shaped crater lake, with waterfalls, natural hot springs, and the volcanic cone of Gunung Baru ("new mountain") budding in its centre. This hidden gem on the mountain's summit is visible only to hardy climbers.

↑ Lake Tamblingan, seen from the edge of the caldera of Gunung Catur

A YEAR IN
BALI AND LOMBOK

JANUARY

△ **Chinese New Year** (Jan/Feb). Observed by Balinese and Sasaks of Chinese descent, Chinese New Year is celebrated with festive dinners, decorations and Chinese *barongsai* lion and dragon dance troupes.

FEBRUARY

△ **Galungan** (19 Feb 2020 – varies). Taking place every 210 days according to the Balinese calendar, this holiday marks the descent of ancestral spirits and Balinese deities to earth.

Bau Nyale Festival (Feb/Mar). Lombok's most popular festival takes place on the beaches around Kuta when thousands of colourful sea worms are washed ashore. The worms are eaten and there is traditional dance and music.

MAY

△ **Takbir Parade** (May/Jun 2019 – varies). The people of Lombok hold a parade to celebrate the end of Ramadan. It is unique to the island.

JUNE

△ **Bali Arts Festival** (mid-Jun–mid-Jul). A month-long festival of Balinese artistic traditions and culture takes place in Denpasar. There are shows of traditional and contemporary dance, shadow puppetry, concerts and art exhibitions.

SEPTEMBER

△ **Senggigi Festival** (early Sep). A four-day celebration of Lombok's art and culture, with street theatre, traditional music and dance, and handicrafts and street-food stalls.

Balinale International Film Festival (late Sep). This week-long festival has a packed programme of award-winning films and movie premieres showcasing Indonesia's best talent.

OCTOBER

△ **Ubud Writers and Readers Festival** (early Oct). Attracting literature enthusiasts from all over the world, this festival provides intellectual and sensory stimulation via interviews, readings, poetry slams and book launches.

Nusa Dua Fiesta (mid-Oct). A week of art exhibitions, theatre performances, fashion shows and food bazaars.

MARCH

△ **Pengrupukan** (*early or mid-Mar*). Lively processions are held all over Bali to drive away the evil spirits with gongs, drums, cymbals and *ogoh-ogoh* papier-mâché monsters on the eve of Nyepi.

Nyepi (*mid-/late Mar*). The Hindu "day of silence" is a public holiday with fasting and meditation. The airport and all businesses are closed, there is no one out on the streets and all lights are extinguished.

APRIL

△ **Bali Spirit Festival** (*early Apr*). This energy-filled festival in Ubud showcases leading practitioners in health, yoga, wellbeing, world music, community programmes and environmental conservation.

Ubud Food Festival (*mid-Apr*). A three-day event to tantalize the taste buds with a huge variety of Balinese and international cuisines.

Gendang Beleq Festival (*mid-Apr*). Big-drum musical troupes gather all over Lombok to accompany colourful dances.

JULY

△ **Stick Fighting Festival** (*Jul*). Senggigi is the best place to see this Lombok event where men compete with wooden sticks and shields to show off their strength and agility to the accompaniment of traditional music.

Bali Kite Festival (*Jul/Aug*). Traditional giant kites, up to 4 x 10 m (13 x 33 ft) in size, are made and flown in competitions by teams from different villages.

AUGUST

△ **Independence Day** (*17 Aug*). This national holiday marks Indonesia's freedom from colonialism. People decorate their houses in red and white and display the national flag. Children participate in fun games.

Ubud Village Jazz Festival (*mid-Aug*). Jazz legends and rising stars from Indonesia and all over the world perform at this two-day festival.

NOVEMBER

△ **Makepung Buffalo Races** (*Jul–Nov*). The Jembrana Cup Finals of the buffalo races take place twice-monthly from July to November near Negara in West Bali.

DECEMBER

△ **Mulang Pekelem** (*Dec*). Hindus in Lombok make a full-moon pilgrimage to Lake Segara Arak in Mount Rinjani's crater.

Perang Topat (*Dec*). Taking place at the Pura Lingsar temple in Lombok, Hindus and Muslims pray for another year of good crops before engaging in a frivolous rice-snack food fight.

A BRIEF
HISTORY

The islands of Bali and Lombok have been battered by powerful empires and conflict, and interactions between them have often been turbulent. Bali has been inhabited for millennia; archaeological discoveries date back 3,000 years. However, little is known about Lombok prior to the 17th century.

The Majapahit Empire

Bali maintained its independence from the kingdoms of East Java until the late 14th century, when it came under the Javanese political sphere. The Javanese Majapahit Empire was a golden era in Bali and saw the birth of Hindu-Javanese traditions of architecture, literature, painting, sculpture and the performing arts. After the collapse of the Majapahit empire in 1515, Bali was united in 1550 under King Batu Renggong, the ruler of Gelgel near Klungkung, and Hindu culture continued to flourish with a boom in temple building and the associated crafts of sculpture and woodcarving.

1 18th-century Dutch map of Bali and Lombok.

2 Pura Maospahit statue, Denpasar, capital of the Majapahit kingdom.

3 Dutch engraving of the Balinese king and his entourage, 1597.

4 1894 photograph taken in Lombok at the time of the Dutch invasion.

Timeline of events

1293
Majapahit kingdom established

1343
Majapahit invasion of Bali by Javanese ruler and general Gajah Mada, who defeated the king in Bedulu

Early 1500s
Hindu-Javanese priests and artisans emigrate to Bali seeking exile from Islamic empires dominating Java

1597
The first Dutch trading ships arrive in Bali searching for spices. The Western world receives fascinating reports about the island

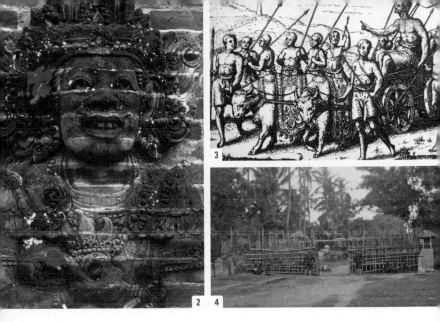

Dutch Rule

The late 16th century brought the first European ships to Bali. The Dutch made claims to the island at this time but were greeted with much hostility. From 1710 onwards, however, the Dutch began to take control, and by 1849 northern and eastern Bali were under Dutch rule. It took three campaigns and more than 60 years to shatter the Balinese defences and morale – campaigns in which the Dutch achieved neither victory nor glory. The most significant events were the suicidal *puputan* in 1906 and 1908, where the royal households presented themselves to the invading Dutch officers and rapidly committed mass suicide. From then onwards the Dutch ruled more leniently.

The Dutch first visited Lombok in 1674 and settled the eastern half while leaving the western half to be ruled by a Balinese-Hindu dynasty. A revolt ended in 1894 with the annexation of the entire island to the Dutch East Indies. For the Lombok people, colonialism meant abject poverty, heavy taxation and the exportation of their food produce, resulting in a famine that tormented the island for nearly half a century.

↑ Statue of Gajah Mada, ruler of the Hindu empire of Majapahit

1894
Dutch conquest of the whole of Lombok; Mataram is destroyed

1906
Dutch attack Badung; royal court commits mass ritual suicide; Bali's Tabanan kingdom surrenders

1908
Mass suicide by royal family in Klungkung; Dutch control all of Bali

1917
Devastating earthquake hits Bali; Gunung Batur erupts, almost completely destroying Batur village

The Golden Age of Travel

The 1920s brought the beginnings of organized tourism to Bali, with bohemians, artists, writers and musicians drawn to its exotic beauty and culture. A number of foreign artists, including the influential Russian-born German primitivist painter Walter Spies, settled on the island and spurred the growth of Balinese art.

Pre-World War II tourists arrived mainly by sea, landing in Singaraja on the north coast or Padang Bai in the southeast. By 1930, up to 100 visitors per month were arriving; it was during this decade that the ferry service between Banyuwangi and Gilimanuk was started up by two enterprising Germans, and a road was built connecting Gilimanuk to Denpasar. Air travel became possible in 1938, but it was very risky. The first survey flight made by the Royal Netherlands Indies Airways (KNILM) crashed into Mount Batukaru, and the first airport, built on the Bukit Peninsula, was too dangerous for landing except in the calmest weather. In 1938 a new airport was built at Tuban on the site of the present airport, and Bali became an overnight stop on the weekly KNILM flights to Australia and Makassar.

THE LAST PARADISE

Early images of Bali by Dutch illustrator W O J Nieuwendamp and German photographer Gregor Krause inspired Westerners to visit the island. Some visitors stayed on more permanently, settling mainly in Ubud and Sanur, and presented to the outside world an image of Bali as "the island of the gods" where "everyone is an artist".

Timeline of events

1920

Westerners start visiting Bali, promoting the concept of Bali as "paradise"

1928

Opening of the first international hotel, the Bali Hotel, in Denpasar

1936

Opening of the first hotel on Bali's Kuta Beach, the Kuta Beach Hotel

1942

Japanese invasion; Dutch withdraw from the archipelago

World War II

In February 1942, with the spread of World War II, a small force of Japanese soldiers landed at Sanur and took over from the demoralized Dutch garrison. In May 1942, the fleet sailed into Lombok. The Dutch defenders were soon defeated and the island occupied. The victorious Japanese ruled Bali and Lombok for three years, very much in accordance with the already established Dutch system. They did not actively intervene in Balinese affairs, but the effects of their enforced requisition of rice and foodstuffs were far-reaching and by the end of the war, the people of Bali and Lombok were suffering severe hardship, facing both famine and epidemics. On 17 August 1945, the first president of Indonesia Sukarno and prime minister Mohammad Hatta declared Indonesia to be an independent nation and the remaining Japanese withdrew. However, the Dutch wanted their colony back; they tried to reassert control but were met with a fight against 95 Indonesian Nationalist fighters led by Gusti Ngurah Rai at Marga village, Tabanan, which led to the last *puputan* in Balinese history. The Dutch finally recognized Indonesia's independence in 1949.

1 Poster for the Bali Hotel by Willem Gerard Hofke, 1920s.

2 The Dutch Reoccupation, 1946.

3 Declaration of Independence by President Sukarno, 1945.

Did You Know?

The 1942 USS *Liberty* shipwreck off Tulamben, Bali, is an interesting and easy dive site *(p139)*.

1945

Japan surrenders; Sukarno becomes president of Indonesia

1946

The Dutch return; Gusti Ngurah Rai and 95 guerrilla fighters massacred by the Dutch

1949

The musical *South Pacific* opens on Broadway. The song *Bali Hai* creates a tropical cliché of Bali

1956

Sukarno dismantles parliamentary democracy and ends free enterprise

Independence

Transition from colonialism to independence was not easy, and by 1956 the whole of Indonesia, led by the charismatic President Sukarno, was undergoing a tumultuous period. Economic conditions had seriously deteriorated and the Communist Party was growing in power. When Bali's volcano, Gunung Agung, erupted in 1963, it added further anguish, killing 1,600 people and displacing 100,000. Massive areas of arable land and crops were ruined, causing food shortages that lasted for months afterwards. The debris from the erupted volcano was later used to build hotels during the tourism boom. In late 1965, the Communist Party staged an abortive coup d'état in Jakarta, and reprisals began all over Indonesia as the Nationalists set out to extinguish all traces of Communism. Bali and Lombok both became scenes of incredible violence, with mass killings of Communist sympathizers and ethnic Chinese.

Tourism, Conflicts and Natural Disasters

When Suharto became president in 1967, Indonesia became open to foreign affairs again. Fortunately, rather than destroy

① Smoke emanating from Gunung Agung volcano on Bali in 1963. ↑

② Tourists lounging under colourful umbrellas and on beanbags on Kuta Beach, Bali.

③ Surfers carrying surfboards on Bali's Kuta Beach at sunset.

Timeline of events

1963
Gunung Agung erupts catastrophically, killing 1,600 and leaving 100,000 homeless

1965–66
Controversial attempted coup; anti-Communist massacres follow - at least 500,000 are killed in Bali and Lombok

1967
Suharto replaces Sukarno as President of Indonesia

1971
Mass tourism programme launched by Indonesian government

1986
Opening of Nusa Dua's luxury tourist enclave of resorts

Bali's unique history and culture, the Suharto regime saw the merits in opening up Bali to tourism. In the 1990s it became one of the most prosperous places in Indonesia. However, in comparison to Bali's glitz and glamour, Lombok always came a poor second. By the end of the decade, corruption in Indonesia had become widespread, the country's economy faltered and ethnic conflicts erupted.

In early 2000, militant Islamists in Lombok attacked Chinese, Christian and Balinese-owned buildings in a spasm of violence that left dozens dead, resulting in a downturn in Lombok's fledgling tourism boom. Bali was also disturbed tragically in October 2002, when bombs planted by militant Islamists exploded in Kuta, killing over 200 people. A further series of bombs went off in Jimbaran and Kuta in 2005, killing 20 people. In July and August 2018, several earthquakes caused catastrophic damage to north Lombok and the Gili Islands, killing 550 people, and injuring 1,500. All of these incidents temporarily affected tourism, yet history tells that Bali and Lombok's resilient cultures, which have so far survived colonialism as well as natural and political disasters, will continue to flourish.

↑ Red roses in the sand at the bomb blast scene in Jimbaran Bay, Bali, 2005

1998
Economic crisis causes riots in Jakarta; President Suharto resigns

2000
Rioting in Lombok; hundreds of Chinese, Christian and Balinese homes, churches and businesses are looted and burned

2017
Gunung Agung becomes active; villagers evacuated

2018
Earthquakes strike Lombok, killing over 550

EXPERIENCE

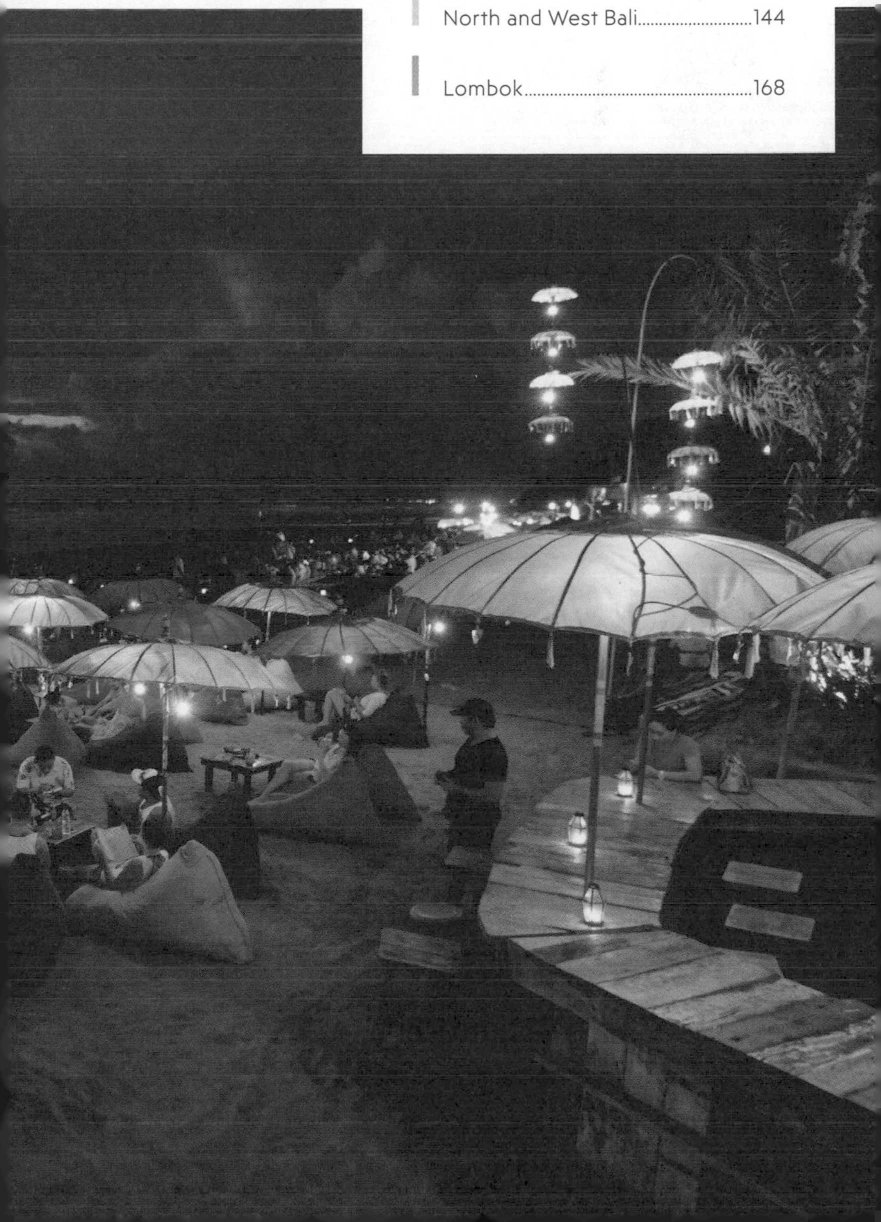

SOUTH BALI AND THE BUKIT PENINSULA

An enticing blend of history, culture and tourism, South Bali offers many contrasts. Travellers started visiting the beaches here after the first surfers arrived in the 1960s. The sea is never far away in South Bali. Surfers come for the waves, divers and snorkellers for the reefs and underwater life. Everyone comes here for the beach life, which has few rivals in Asia or further afield. Despite modern development, temples and village communities still maintain their cultural and artistic traditions.

At the heart of South Bali is Denpasar, the island's provincial capital since 1958 and today a busy city. Denpasar used to be a royal capital – the kingdom of Badung dominated the southern part of Bali from the late 18th to the beginning of the 20th century – and its heritage can still be seen in several older buildings.

The Bukit Peninsula in the far south has some of Bali's very best beaches and top surfing spots, and the famous cliff-top temple Pura Luhur Uluwatu, with its spectacular view of the ocean.

Tanah Lot

Munggu

Gaji

Ubung Kaja

NORTH AND
WEST BALI
p144

Ubung

Cemagi

Kangkang

Kayutulang

Kerobokan
Raja

Pemecutan
Kaja

Pererenan

7
CANGGU

Anyarbelodan

Kerobokan

Padangsambian

Semor

Umalas

Tegal Kertha

Kerobokan
Klod

Padangsambian
Klod

Petitenget

Pengubengan

Taman
Basangkasa

Batannyuh

6
SEMINYAK

Geladag

Pemecutan

4
KUTA AND LEGIAN

Pelasa

Sakah

*Kuta
Bay*

Rangkansa

5
SOUTH KUTA
BEACH

Indian Ocean

Ngurah Rai
International
Airport

BALI MANDARA TOLL ROAD

Kedonganan

9
BENOA
HARBOUR

*Jimbaran
Bay*

11
JIMBARAN

Tegalwangi

Kuta Selatan

Mumbul

BINGIN BEACH
15

Simpangan

GARUDA WISNU
KENCANA CULTURAL
PARK

Anca

PADANG PADANG
BEACH
13

12

ULUWATU **16**

UNGASAN
17

Banket

Bukit   Peninsula

1
PURA LUHUR
ULUWATU

14
PECATU

Kutuh

0 kilometres   2

0 miles   2

N
↑

CENTRAL BALI
p90

SOUTH BALI
AND THE BUKIT
PENINSULA

SOUTH BALI AND THE BUKIT PENINSULA

Must Sees

1. Pura Luhur Uluwatu
2. Denpasar
3. Sanur
4. Kuta and Legian

Experience More

5. South Kuta Beach
6. Seminyak
7. Canggu
8. Pulau Serangan
9. Benoa Harbour
10. Tanjung Benoa
11. Jimbaran
12. Garuda Wisnu Kencana Cultural Park
13. Padang Padang Beach
14. Pecatu
15. Bingin Beach
16. Uluwatu
17. Ungasan
18. Nusa Dua
19. Nusa Penida
20. Nusa Lembongan
21. Nusa Ceningan

Nusa Penida

Area of main map

0 kilometres   15

0 miles   15

N

The three-tiered *meru*,
dedicated to Nirartha,
who achieved enlightenment
while meditating here →

❶ 🎨

PURA LUHUR ULUWATU

🅐D5 🏠 End of Jalan Uluwatu, Uluwatu 🚍
🕐 6am–7pm daily

Not only one of Bali's most sacred places of worship
but also one of the most beautiful examples of
Balinese architecture, Pura Luhur Uluwatu, on Bali's
extreme southwesterly tip, is one of a series of sea
temples dedicated to the guardian spirits of the ocean.

The temple's history is shrouded in mystery but it is believed to
have been founded in the 11th century by the architect-priest
Mpu Kuturan. Five hundred years later, the temple was rebuilt
by the reformer-priest Dang Hyang Nirartha, who was the
founder of the Shaivite priesthood in Bali. Nirartha chose Pura
Uluwatu as his last earthly abode.

Part of the temple fell into the sea just before the *puputan*
(ritual suicide) of the royal court of Badung after the Dutch
invasion of 1906 *(p55)*. This was regarded as an omen of the
impending disaster. In the late 1990s, some of the shrines
were set on fire by lightning, which was interpreted to augur
the economic and political troubles of the time.

Until the beginning of the 20th century, admission to the
temple was forbidden to anyone except for the princes of
Badung. Visitors should cover their shoulders and knees;
sarongs and sashes can be rented for a nominal fee.

↑ Hindu pilgrims gathering at Pura Luhur Uluwatu
for a ceremony of prayers and worship

Did You Know?

The temple is sacred to
fishermen, who come
to pray to the sea
goddess, Dewi Laut.

↑ Pura Luhur Uluwatu,
commanding a glorious
position on a cliff top

Layout of the Temple

The inner sanctuaries of the temple are off limits to those who are not praying. However, much can be seen from the outside. The extremely hard, grey coral walls have enabled the temple and its well-preserved decorative stone carvings to survive for centuries. The outermost gate is a *candi bentar* or split gate whose inner sides are tipped with carved wings. This gate marks the spot where the realm of man meets that of the gods.

The temple's layout follows the tripartite pattern of godly, human and demonic worlds in the form of three courtyards. Towering over the central courtyard is an enormous arched gate guarded by statues of the elephant-headed god, Ganesha – the remover of obstacles and the god of knowledge. Kala's monstrous face peers out from above the gate, while his hands reach out beside his head to catch any evil spirits foolish enough to attempt to sneak in. As the creator of light and a leader in the underworld, Kala's role is to balance unequal forces. Behind the main pagoda of the temple's small inner sanctum, a limestone statue of a Brahman priest, believed to be Dang Hyang Nirartha, surveys the Indian Ocean.

💬 INSIDER TIP
Visiting

The best time to visit the temple is the late afternoon when the sea breezes rise. Monkeys inhabit this area so keep your valuables out of sight. A Kecak dance performance is held in the temple grounds at sunset every day.

→
Illustration of the Pura Luhur Uluwatu, perched on a cliff top

Three-tiered meru

The inner courtyard is reserved for worshippers.

↑ Guardian statue of Hanuman, a mythical Hindu monkey figure

These stepped paths along the cliff rise 200 m (650 ft) above the sea.

Candi bentar (split gate) ↑
forming the main entrance
to the temple

The unusual arched main gate
has the shape of Meru, the
Cosmic Mountain of Hinduism.
Surmounting it are three finials
and a Kala head – a fanged
demon with bulging eyes,
believed to ward off evil spirits.

↑ The arched stone
gate leading to the
inner courtyard

These Ganesha – elephant-
headed guardian statues,
wearing a belt with a clasp
in the form of a Cyclops –
are masterpieces of
Balinese sculpture.

The jero tengah, or central
courtyard, offers spectacular
views of the sunset.

At the top of the stairs leading
to the temple is a candi bentar
(split gate), decorated with
elaborate carvings.

The astasai is a
shrine for festival
offerings.

This shrine is dedicated to
Dang Hyang Nirartha,
with images of Brahma
and Vishnu.

The bale tajuk are
shrines for the spiritual
guardians of Nirartha.

2

DENPASAR

E4 From Kuta, Sanur and Nusa Dua Jalan Raya Puputan 41, Renon; (0361) 235 600

Denpasar is Bali's bustling provincial capital. Some older buildings predate the Dutch invasion of 1906 (*p55*), and there are still some white-walled, red-tiled structures from colonial times. On the streets are several statues of heroes of Indonesia's struggle for independence. Around the main street, Jalan Gajah Mada, are shop-houses built by Chinese, Arab and Indian traders.

① Pasar Badung

Jalan Gajah Mada
Daily

This lively market is full of colour and excitement; sellers from all over Bali do a brisk trade all day. The extensive flower section is not to be missed – exotic blossoms used in religious offerings (*p46*) are a major commodity on Bali.

The fruit, vegetable and fish market is full of spectacular tropical harvests. Bargains can be found among the stalls offering textiles, mats, basket and traditional dancers' costumes.

② Kumbasari Art Market

Jalan Gajah Mada 5am-5pm daily

Located just across the river from Pasar Badung, this four-storey rabbit warren of small shops specializes in handicrafts, souvenirs, artifacts, clothes, fabrics, gold work and other artistic goods.

The ground floor sells spices, ceremonial pots and jars, baskets and temple offerings. The first floor is dedicated to budget clothing, traditional textiles and random handicrafts. Art shops featuring handicrafts from Lombok, as well as Balinese woodcarvings, can be found on the second floor. Check out the art shop on the mezzanine between the second and third floor, where the paintings are very reasonably priced. The third floor features more art shops, and on the fourth floor you'll find internationally designed products.

③ Jalan Gajah Mada

Several interesting Chinese apothecaries with an array of herbal medicines can be found on this busy street. One of the largest is Toko Saudara. Other stores sell electronics, sporting goods, handicrafts, batik and *ikat* textiles. Many traders of Arab and Indian descent have businesses here.

INSIDER TIP
Tranquil Escape

Although a hectic city, Denpasar has quieter leafy streets in the Renon business district. The Bajra Sandhi Monument, commemorating the island's struggle against the Dutch, offers panoramic views.

← Fruit and spice stalls at the sprawling Pasar Badung market

④ Taman Puputan

🅐 Jalan Udayana and Jalan Surapati

Puputan translates as "suicidal fight to the end", and this large square in the middle of town (once the site of Denpasar's palace) has a huge bronze statue which commemorates the heroic *puputan* of the rajahs against the Dutch invaders of 1906 (*p55*). The monument portrays a Balinese family brandishing weapons. The woman holds jewels as the royal Balinese women are said to have thrown their jewellery at the Dutch soldiers in protest.

Nowadays the square is much more peaceful, making a pleasant green oasis amid the bustle and noise of Denpasar.

⑤ Catur Muka

🅐 Northwest corner of Taman Puputan

At the intersection of four streets, on the traffic island adjacent to Taman Puputan, is a representation of Brahma, the four-headed Hindu god of creation, who is shown in the form of a stone statue 20 m (65 ft) tall, dating from the 1970s. The name means "four faces". The landmark statue was created by the famous artist I Gusti Nyoman Lempad.

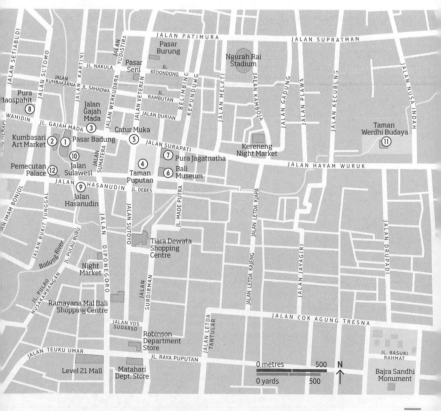

⑥ ♿

Bali Museum

📍Jalan Mayor Wisnu 1,
on east side of Taman
Puputan 📞(0361) 222 680
🕐8am-3pm Mon-Thu, 8am-
12:30pm Fri 🚫Public hols

The Bali Museum is the oldest on the island, and has more than 10,000 exhibits in several pavilions. There are archaeological finds dating back to the megalithic period, dance masks, textiles woven in the Bali Aga villages, crafts, ceremonial objects and displays on Bali's architectural styles and theatrical arts. The exterior walls, decorative split gates and courtyards have been structured in the classic Denpasar palace style, while the Tabanan (theatrical masks and musical instruments), Karangasem (sculptures, woodcarvings and paintings) and Buleleng (textiles) pavilions are built in the style of the regencies after which they are named.

Ignore the advances of unofficial guides and work your own way around the museum buildings. Most displays are labelled in English.

SHOPPING IN DENPASAR

Jalan Sulawesi is Denpasar's fabric street, devoted to cloth of all descriptions. Most of the stores are long and narrow lock-ups, open at the front, dimly lit and piled high with hundreds of rolls of cloth. Try to shake off the commission hunters who will latch on to you and offer to be your guide. Jalan Hasanudin is the locale for Bali's gold shops, featuring Balinese gold jewellery. If you change your mind after your purchase, most of the shops will allow you to return the item (supported by the guarantee certificate) and to get your money back, less 5–10 per cent. Most shops open daily from 9am until 9pm.

⑦

Pura Jagatnatha

📍Taman Puputan, Jalan Letkol Wisnu 🕐Daily

This temple was built in the 1970s for the worship of Sang Hyang Widhi Wasa, the Supreme God. It is crowded on the full and new moons, and on Kajeng Kliwon, an auspicious day for cleansing the mind, which falls every 15 days in the Balinese calendar. The temple has a tall *padmasana* ("lotus throne") shrine with an empty seat at the top open to the sky.

⑧

Pura Maospahit

📍Jalan Sutomo, Grenceng 🚫To the public

Dating to the 13th–15th centuries, when the Majapahit ruled over Bali (p54), this temple was badly damaged in an earthquake in 1917 and has been heavily restored since. The style of the statuary, the red brickwork and the restrained ornamentation developed during the Majapahit period are delightful. Although the temple is closed to visitors, the interesting architecture can be admired from outside.

⑨ 🛍

Jalan Hasanudin

Shops selling a vast selection of gold jewellery in Balinese, Indonesian and Western designs line this street.

___

⑩ 🛍

Jalan Sulawesi

This three-block stretch houses myriad fabrics and textiles. Everything from cheap batiks to imported silks and brocades can be found here. This is where the Balinese come to buy their temple clothing, and the delicate lace used for *kebaya* (a traditional tight-fitting ladies' blouse).

___

⑪

Taman Werdhi Budaya

🏠 Jalan Nusa Indah
📞 (0361) 227 176 🕐 8am–5pm Tue–Sun 🚫 Public hols

Also known as the Bali Arts Centre, this is an attractive if under-used complex with extensive gardens, an art

museum, several indoor theatres and an outdoor amphitheatre. There are frequent dance and music performances, but no set programme.

The centre is a good place to come to during the heat of the day. Its permanent collection of sculptures and paintings reflects the art world of the 1970s and 1980s, and more recent works are shown in rotating exhibitions.

Information and events can be found listed in the *Bali Post* newspaper and tourist magazines.

___

⑫ 🎭

Pemecutan Palace

🏠 Jalan Thamrin 25
📞 (0361) 423 491

Resting in the thick of the old city, Pemecutan Palace was the first of Denpasar's royal houses to open its doors to visitors. It is still inhabited by the current king of Denpasar.

← The tall lotus throne shrine in the Pura Jagatnatha temple

↑ Shop selling a wide range of textiles on Jalan Sulawesi

The palace has ornate and classic architecture and beautiful royal family shrines dating back to the 17th century. It consists of two main compounds – the living quarters and the place of worship. In the spacious outer courtyard there is a bell-tower and a gamelan pavilion. An elaborately carved gate leads to the middle courtyard, which is home to a *balairung*, or large hall, where the king still holds court, and there is an open stage for dance and theatre peformances.

↑ Detail of a sculpture in the grounds of Pemecutan Palace

3 🍴 💻 🛍️

SANUR

🅰️ E4 ℹ️ Denpasar; (0361) 754 092 🚌🚤 To Nusa Penida and Nusa Lembongan

Bali's longest-established resort, Sanur has a simple layout and tranquil atmosphere that appeal to those seeking a relaxed holiday with the convenience and facilities of a beach resort.

① Pura Desa

🅰️ Jalan Hang Tuah 🕐 Daily

This fine village temple was probably built early in the 20th century, although its brickwork has been restored since. It is in Sanur's oldest neighbourhood, which is famous for the spiritual power of its priests.

② Pura Belanjong

🅰️ Jalan Danau Poso 🕐 Daily

In this plain-looking temple is an ancient stone column, the Prasasti Blanjong. On it is carved the oldest edict so far found in Bali (AD 914). The inscription is written in a form of Sanskrit, although it is not all decipherable. It suggests Sanur was a lively trading port more than 1,000 years ago.

③ Sanur Beach

The beach runs almost the full length of the town; along much of it is a paved walk. Offshore, enormous breakers crash into a reef. The calm waters between the reef and the white sands are good for swimming except at low tide and are excellent for exploring marine life. Beyond the reef

↑ The Pura Belanjong temple, housing a stone Sanskrit column

the currents are strong. Activities include diving, fishing trips and an evening sail on a *jukung*, a traditional outrigger.

④ 🍴 💻

Beach Promenade
A well-maintained paved promenade, including a 5-km (3-mile) cycle path, runs next

↑ The rising sun reflected in the calm morning waters at Sanur Beach

to the sandy beach, saved from erosion by an impressive landscaping and conservation project that has also safeguarded the coral reef. Curved stone jetties extend at intervals, each with a bale pavilion on the end where fishermen linger. The promenade is also home to two art markets, while the northern end marks the departure point for boats to Nusa Lembongan and Nusa Penida.

EAT

Spice by Chris Salans
French cooking techniques are applied to local ingredients, creating surprising flavours which showcase Indonesia's roots, herbs and spices.

🏠 Jalan Danau Tamblingan 140
📞 (0361) 449 0411

Ⓡⓟ Ⓡⓟ Ⓡⓟ

Kayu Manis
This gem offers an exceptional menu of Western and Asian fusion dishes. Reservations recommended.

🏠 Jalan Tandakan 6
📞 (0361) 289 410

Ⓡⓟ Ⓡⓟ Ⓡⓟ

Three Monkeys
A wide variety of tasty, innovative dishes from all over the world is served here, with an emphasis on Mediterranean and Asian-inspired cuisine.

🏠 Jalan Danau Tamblingan 📞 (0361) 286 002

Ⓡⓟ Ⓡⓟ Ⓡⓟ

⑤

Pura Segara

🏠 Jalan Segara Ayu, or from Sanur Beach 🕐 Daily

Set in the grounds of Segara Village Hotel, but accessible to the public, this is one of the best of several beach temples built of coral. The pyramid shape of the offering houses is unique to Sanur, suggesting origins in prehistoric times.

⑥

Museum Le Mayeur

🏠 Jalan Hang Tuah, via Grand Inna Bali Beach Hotel 📞 (0361) 286 201 🕐 8am-3:30pm daily (to 12:30pm Fri)

Built in the 1930s by Adrien-Jean Le Mayeur, a Belgian painter and one of Sanur's first European residents, the house became a museum and gallery on the artist's death in 1958. About 80 of Le Mayeur's paintings are on display. Many depict a colourful, idealized portrayal of Balinese life. Le Mayeur's wife, the Balinese dancer Ni Polok, is the subject of several paintings.

⑦

Bali Orchid Garden

🏠 Jalan Bypass Tohpati, Kasamba 1 🕐 8am-6pm daily 🌐 baliorchid gardens.com

This beautiful botanical garden is a serene tropical haven, with a huge variety of orchids that bloom throughout the year. For those keen to take home a piece of paradise, many of the flowers are also available to buy.

↑ The long shadows of the sunset over the sands of Kuta Beach

④ 🍴 💻 🛍️

KUTA AND LEGIAN

🅐E4 🚌 ℹ️ Jalan Raya Kuta and Jalan Pantai Kuta 2; (0361) 754 092

Somewhat loud and busy, with a world-famous resort strip, Kuta and Legian are the most developed visitor destinations in Bali. The streets are lined with hotels, bars, restaurants, cafés, nightclubs and shops, while the long and sandy beach is popular with surfers. Besides the beach and water sports, the principal attractions are shopping and nightlife.

①
Kuta and Legian Beach

The beach is flat and sandy, and stretches for over 3 km (2 miles), backed by some sizeable hotels. Hawkers sell their wares and refreshments are available all day long. Surfboards can be rented – this is a good place for the novice surfer, although you should watch out for the rip tides. Because of currents, swimmers should stay between the safety flags. Kuta Beach becomes Legian Beach north of Jalan Melasti.

Extending north from Kuta Beach, Legian Beach is a lovely stretch of white sand and has a slightly more relaxed ambience than Kuta. Legian's labyrinth of backstreets offers a wide range of family-friendly accommodation options close to the beach.

② 🛍️
Poppies Lanes I & II

These two narrow lanes are lined with small shops, stalls, hotels and bars. One of the first hotels to open in Kuta was Poppies, from which the lanes took their name. The network of alleys in this part of Kuta offers a refuge from the traffic, pollution and noise of the main streets.

③ 🍴 🛍️
Jalan Legian

This is the commercial artery of Kuta, running parallel with the beach. At the southern end is Bemo Corner, a busy intersection. The street connects Kuta and Seminyak. Jalan Legian is lined with restaurants, surf stores, art shops, fashion boutiques and massage and reflexology parlours. One of Bali's primary nightlife hubs, the street is full of pubs, bars and nightclubs – some, such as The Bounty, Vi Ai Pi and Sky Garden Rooftop Lounge nightclubs, are landmarks in themselves.

Did You Know?

Tourism in Bali began on Kuta Beach in the 1930s.

④
Bali Bombing Memorial

🏠 Jalan Legian, Kuta

This elegant stone monument is dedicated to those who lost their lives in the terrorist attack in Kuta on 12 October 2002. Built on the site of the destroyed Paddy's Pub, it features a marble plaque bearing the nationalities and names of the 202 victims. The fatalities included 88 Australians, 38 Indonesians and 23 British, as well as victims from 19 other countries. An additional 209 people were injured. The first bomb was detonated at Paddy's Pub at 11:05pm, causing patrons to flee the building; 20 seconds later, a powerful car bomb exploded outside the Sari Club on the opposite side of the street.

⑤ 🍴 🖥 🛍
Kuta Square

🕐 9am–10pm daily

Bali's original shopping arcade consists of a hotchpotch of glass-fronted shops, including a Matahari department store, a jewellery emporium, a large, high-end batik outlet, souvenir shops, local designer boutiques and sports shops. Surfwear concept stores include Dreamland Surf, Kuta Lines, Quiksilver, Volcom, Rip Curl and Billabong. Prominent international outlets such as Armani, Gucci, Versace and Donna Karan can also be found here. There is some speculation as to whether or not all of the designer goods are the genuine article, but price is usually the best guideline. There is also a good range of restaurants.

> Extending north from Kuta Beach, Legian Beach is a lovely stretch of white sand and has a slightly more relaxed ambience than Kuta.

EAT

Kori Restaurant & Bar
Dine on delicious Indonesian and international dishes in a serene garden setting, complete with cabanas and lotus ponds.

🏠 Jalan Legian, Jalan Poppies II, Kuta
Ⓦ korirestaurant.co.id

Ⓡ Ⓡ Ⓡ

Poppies Restaurant
A Kuta institution, Poppies serves exquisite seafood and Indonesian and international cuisine among flowers and waterfalls.

🏠 Poppies Lane 1/19, Jalan Legian, Kuta
Ⓦ poppies bali.com

Ⓡ Ⓡ Ⓡ

Rosso Vivo Dine & Lounge
This delightful Italian eatery, with ocean views and comfortable lounge seating, serves a wide range of pizzas, pastas and desserts.

🏠 Jalan Pantai Kuta, Kuta Ⓦ rossovivo bali.com

Ⓡ Ⓡ Ⓡ

Made's Warung
Established in 1969, this is the most famous restaurant in Kuta. It serves Indonesian, Western, Thai and Japanese cuisine.

🏠 Jalan Pantai Kuta, Banjar Pande Mas, Kuta
Ⓦ madeswarung. com/kuta

Ⓡ Ⓡ Ⓡ

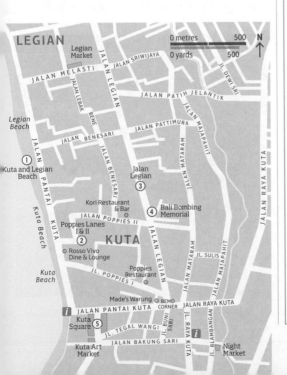

EXPERIENCE MORE

EAT

Warung Damar

Bathed in the glow of coloured lanterns at night, this garden-restaurant offers authentic dishes from around the Indonesian archipelago.

🅰E4 ⬛Jalan Kartika Plaza, South Kuta 🌐warung damar-bali.com

⒭⒭⒭

Queen's of India

High-quality Indian cuisine here includes tandoori dishes, curries and biryanis.

🅰E4 ⬛Jalan Kartika Plaza, South Kuta 🌐bali.queens tandoor.com

⒭⒭⒭

Taco Beach Grill

The delightful Taco Beach Grill serves innovative California-style Mexican food, fused with Balinese dishes such as *babi guling* burritos.

🅰E4 ⬛Jalan Kunti I 8, Seminyak 🌐bali. tacobeachgrill.com

⒭⒭⒭

Mama San

Asian comfort food is served in this eatery with a Shanghai 1920s-era vibe.

🅰E4 ⬛Jalan Raya Kerobokan 135, Seminyak 🌐mamasanbali.com

⒭⒭⒭

---

5 🍴 🍽 🏛

South Kuta Beach

🅰E4 ⬛From Kuta 🛈Kuta; (0361) 754 092

The South Kuta Beach area (also known as Tuban) stretches south from Kuta Square along Jalan Kartika Plaza, towards the airport boundary. Land reclamation projects have restored the beach to its former glory, and massive investments have resulted in upgrades and renovations to provide elegant accommodation and world-class facilities just steps from the sand. This family-oriented area provides a broad choice of international accommodation options, ranging from simple home-stays to mid-range hotels and five-star resorts, many of which have multiple dining venues, swanky rooftop bars and luxurious spas.

The white sandy beach has a 3-km (2-mile) boardwalk, which is great for strolling,

jogging or cycling, in between stopping off at the many shops, restaurants and cafés. Visitors can enjoy an eclectic array of restaurants offering a variety of cuisines, as well as the popular beachfront Discovery Mall and Lippo Mall with its three-theatre

↑ A boy playing with the wares at his father's kite stall on South Kuta Beach

↑ People gathering to watch the sunset on the beach at Seminyak

Cinemaxx complex, which presents daily screenings of the latest Hollywood blockbusters. Both of these modern shopping malls are air-conditioned, providing a welcome respite from the heat. There is also a superb selection of independent shops, as well as the Kuta Art Market on Jalan Bakung Sari, plenty of indulgent day spas, and numerous bars and nightlife venues offering live music, cabaret shows and the opportunity to dance the night away. Family recreation options include **Waterbom Park**, featuring a whole host of exhilarating waterslides that will get the heart racing, as well as a children's area, a lazy river, massage facilities, restaurants and shady cabanas surrounded by tropical gardens.

The beach is the departure point for surfers wishing to make their way to the break at Kuta Reef; fishermen with motorized outriggers can be chartered for the trip.

Waterbom Park
 🛉 Jalan Kartika Plaza Tuban 🆆 waterbombali.com

🌀 🍴 🖥 🛍
Seminyak
Ⓐ E4 🚌 From Kuta 🛈 Kuta; (0361) 754 092

Seminyak extends north of Kuta and Legian. The further north you go, the more peaceful the atmosphere becomes, although Seminyak is a dynamic, major tourist hub. Some good fashion boutiques can be found here, selling stylish clothes made in the region.

The luxurious Oberoi Hotel has lovely gardens overlooking the beach. Further north still, in the Petitenget area, you'll find Potato Head Beachclub, with three bars, three restaurants and an infinity pool , and the glamorous W Retreat, which has pools restaurants and a spa.

A short walk up the beach north of Seminyak is the **Pura Petitenget** ("magic chest") temple, raised some 8 m (26 ft) above road level. Founded by the 16th-century priest Dang Hyang Nirartha, who was the founder of the Shaivite priesthood in Bali, it is one of a series of sea

temples stretching from Pura Luhur Uluwatu on the Bukit Peninsula north to Pura Tanah Lot in Western Bali. Considered one of Bali's most mystically charged temples, it is the site of many important ceremonies.

The area from Seminyak to Kerobokan, 5 km (3 miles) to its north, is a furniture-making centre. Galleries line the main road.

Pura Petitenget
🚹 Jalan Kayu Aya ⊙ Daily

SUNSETS IN SEMINYAK

A popular activity around Seminyak is to gather on the beach in the evening to watch the stunning sunsets of reds, oranges and purples while sipping a cold beer. A good place for this magical experience is the stretch of sand near Pura Petitenget, which tends to be less busy than the main beach.

7 (🍴)(☕)(🛍)

Canggu

🅰D4 🛈Denpasar; (0361) 756 176

A 12-km (seven-mile) drive northwest of Seminyak on the edge of the Badung greenbelt, the villages of Tibubeneng, Berawa, Canggu and Pererenan – collectively known as Canggu – used to be little more than a sleepy coastal district celebrated among the surfing fraternity for its beach breaks. The advent in 2006, however, of the international Canggu Community School led to the area drawing in a more family-oriented and affluent ex-pat community, with real-estate developers competing for the most cherished plots of land.

Canggu has since evolved into Bali's hippest beachside scene, popular for its juice bars, coffee shops, numerous restaurants, and vegan cafés promoting healthy cuisine.

Exercise fanatics can choose between three fitness clubs, a dance studio, copious yoga centres and a couple of surf schools. Finn's Recreation Club offers sports and leisure facilities, including Splash kids' waterpark. Horse lovers who relish a canter along the beach will find three riding stables in the area, while a pulsating nightlife scene can be enjoyed at Canggu's live-music venues.

Other attractions include spas and beauty lounges, fashion boutiques and two beach clubs. Accommodation ranges from opulent holiday villas, beachside resorts and surf camps, to yoga retreats, serviced apartments, eco-hotels and guesthouses. Meanwhile, traditional Balinese village life continues in Canggu as it has always done. Crops are planted and harvested, ritual music is carried on the breeze and temple ceremonies are a common sight.

Did You Know?

In 2018 Canggu was named the fastest-growing beach destination in the world.

EAT

The Shady Shack
This roadside rice-field shack has shaded seating, a shabby-chic vibe and a healthy, meat-free menu.

🅰D4 📍Jl Tanah Barak 57, Canggu ☎(0819) 1639 5087

Ⓡ Ⓡ Ⓡ

Musubi
Elegant café offering Japanese all-day brunch. Delights include burgers and prawn katsu bao buns.

🅰D4 📍Jl Pantai Berawa 6/7, Canggu 🌐musubibali.com

Ⓡ Ⓡ Ⓡ

The Lawn
A two-storey beachfront restaurant with amazing views, The Lawn has a modern Australian menu.

🅰D4 📍Jalan Pura Dalem, Canggu 🌐thelawncanggu.com

Ⓡ Ⓡ Ⓡ

← Surfers heading into the water at a popular spot on Canggu Beach

8 🖊️

Pulau Serangan

🅰️ E4

The island of Serangan is separated from the southern curve of Sanur Beach by a mangrove area known as Suwungwas. It is also known as "Turtle Island" due to being a nesting ground for green sea turtles. The island has been greatly extended and its natural landscape changed by reclamation during construction works for a new development. A causeway links it to mainland Bali. The two original old fishing villages of Ponjok and Dukuh remain. Besides the Balinese Hindus, there is an old Bugis Muslim community whose ancestors migrated here from South Sulawesi in the 1600s.

Pulau Serangan is home to one of the six most sacred temples in Bali – **Pura Sakenan**, located on the westernmost edge of the

island. The temple is said by some to have been founded by the 16th-century reformist priest Dang Hyang Nirartha. Others, however, believe the temple was founded in the 11th century by the Javanese Buddhist priest Mpu Kuturan. Within the inner courtyard is a stepped pyramid built of white coral, reminiscent of temples in Polynesia. During Galungan (p52), a vibrant festival takes place here every 210 days on the temple's anniversary, drawing huge numbers of devotees.

The island is good for watersports, especially surfing on its eastern side. It is also a good vantage point from which to watch vessels returning to Benoa Harbour at the end of the day. There are great views of Nusa Dua, Nusa Lembongan and Nusa Penida islands and beautiful sunsets.

Pura Sakenan
🖊️ 🅰️ Pulau Serangan
🕐 Daily

9 🚌

Benoa Harbour

🅰️ C4 🚌 From Denpasar (shuttle bus services to Benoa from hotels) 🚢 To Lembar on Lombok

Linked to Nusa Dua by a scenic highway across the Benoa Bay, Benoa Harbour will appeal to boat-lovers. Among the commercial and privately owned vessels, there is often an interesting variety of traditional craft from the Indonesian archipelago. These include *pinisi*, broad-beamed sailing cargo boats from South Sulawesi; and brightly coloured fishing boats from Madura, off northeast Java. There is a multitude of boat charters and tours on offer. Day trips to Nusa Lembongan (p89) are recommended, while longer excursions can be taken as far as Komodo and the Lesser Sunda Islands.

Nearby, on the Jalan Bypass Ngurah Rai, is the Mangrove Information Centre (tel 0361 728 966), which aims to preserve the 15 species of coastal mangrove in its natural forest.

→ Balinese fishing boats lined up in Benoa Harbour

EAT

Sundara Bali
This refined beach club becomes a sophisticated restaurant by night offering sushi, Wagyu steaks and seafood.

🅰E4 🏠Four Seasons Resort, Jalan Bukit Permai, Jimbaran 🅦sundarabali.com

(Rp)(Rp)(Rp)

Balique
Brimming with *objets d'art*, Balique offers a mix of Indonesian and European cuisine.

🅰E4 🏠Jalan Raya Uluwatu 39, Jimbaran 🅦balique-restaurant. com

(Rp)(Rp)(Rp)

Cuca
Globally inspired dishes from local ingredients include enticing tapas, fun cocktails and creative desserts.

🅰E4 🏠Jalan Yoga Perkanthi, Jimbaran 🅦cucaflavor.com

(Rp)(Rp)(Rp)

Fat Chow Temple Hill
Serving Chinese, Thai and Asian fusion dishes, this hilltop restaurant has a spectacular view.

🅰E4 🏠Jalan Raya Uluwatu 8D, Jimbaran 📞(0857) 3875 2224

(Rp)(Rp)(Rp)

Seafood Cafés
More than 30 seafood cafés line the beach at Jimbaran Bay, offering grilled seafood feasts.

🅰E4 🏠Pantai Jimbaran

(Rp)(Rp)(Rp)

---

10 🍴 🖥 🛍

Tanjung Benoa

🅰E4 🚌From Nusa Dua 🛈Kuta; (0361) 754 092

Tanjung (meaning "Cape") Benoa is a long, narrow, sandy spit, with a small fishing village built on it. The cape is separated from Benoa Harbour by a narrow stretch of water. The village was once a trading port, and some Chinese and Bugis as well as Balinese still live here. There are several Balinese temples built of carved limestone, and a mosque. At the ancient bright-red Caow Eng Bio Chinese temple, built by sailors and traders on the northern end of the peninsula, fishermen of all religions regularly consult with the fortune-teller in the hope of finding a good catch.

A modern road leads to the tip of the peninsula from Nusa Dua. Hotels, spas and restaurants specializing in grilled seafood line both sides of the road. One quirky landmark is the stone pineapple motif marking the entrance to the Novotel.

A beach restoration project has resulted in a series of picturesque, crescent-shaped stone piers, complete with open-sided gazebos. There are facilities for water sports, such as water-skiing, banana boat rides, fishing and parasailing. Cruise operators offer trips out to sea for snorkelling in waters rich in corals and tropical fish.

---

11 🍴 🛍

Jimbaran

🅰E4 🛈Kuta; (0361) 754 092

A large fishing village and resort, Jimbaran has one of Bali's best beaches. A beautiful arc of white sand lines its bay, which is protected by an unbroken coral reef. The beach is a great place to watch sunsets and has spectacular views. On a clear day the profiles of all Bali's volcanoes and hills are visible from here, including the three peaks of Gunung Batukaru to the west (*p160*), and Gunung Batur (*p120*), Gunung Agung (*p142*), Gunung Abang (*p143*) and Gunung Seraya (*p141*) to the east. The beach offers sailing boats for hire and the waves are good for bodysurfing.

A lively fish market takes place daily from early morning until mid-afternoon along the bay. The daily morning market on Jalan Uluwatu sells superb fresh produce.

The Chinese Buddhist Caow Eng Bio temple in Tanjung Benoa ↑

 Fisherman casting a fishing net off the coast of Jimbaran at sunset ↑

Jimbaran offers a plethora of great places to eat, especially seafood restaurants. The beach is lined with thatch-roofed cafés, where diners choose their fresh seafood, which is then grilled over coconut husks and delivered to the table.

There are no individual buildings of great interest to visit in Jimbaran, but it is a good place for observing local everyday life. A large fishing settlement consisting of simple huts sits near the waterfront. Many of the fishermen are not of Balinese origin, but migrants from the islands of Java and Madura. The brightly painted boats with their impressive bows and sterns can be seen all day long bobbing at anchor in the surf off the coast. As the sun begins to set, the fishing craft set off into the dusk with lamps burning – an unforgettable sight.

A little north of Jimbaran, Kuta Reef is one of Bali's best surfing points. The reef break is just one of the surfing spots in the sea around the Ngurah Rai International Airport and can be reached by chartering an outrigger at Jimbaran.

South of Jimbaran, much of the coast is a series of limestone cliffs interspersed with some of Bali's most luxurious holiday rental villas and boutique hotels.

---

12 🖎 🍽 🖵 🛍

Garuda Wisnu Kencana Cultural Park

🅰 E5 🏠 Jalan Raya Uluwatu, Ungasan 🕗 8am–10pm daily 🌐 gwk-bali.com

This hillside cultural park and event venue, also known simply as GWK, has as its centrepiece an immense statue, completed in 2018, which is visible from a distance of 25 km (15 miles). The 64-m (210-ft) wide structure sits atop a lofty pedestal that brings its total height to 121 m (397 ft), making it one of the largest monumental statues in the world. Sculpted in green copper and brass, it is a beautiful representation of the supreme Hindu god Vishnu, riding on the back of Garuda, the winged messenger, as his trusted companion. Together, Garuda and Vishnu symbolize the harmony between humankind and the environment, as well as the spirituality of Bali.

The statue and park are the concept of the leading Indonesian sculptor Nyoman Nuarta, whose vision was to create an arena for culture and art. Shows of Indonesian and Balinese traditional dance and music take place daily. Venues include the dramatic Lotus Pond outdoor area, enclosed by enormous limestone pillars, the Street Theatre, Plaza Kura-Kura and Indraloka Garden. The complex also has a gallery for art exhibitions, a cinema, a restaurant serving authentic Balinese cuisine and a gift shop with a range of souvenirs and handicrafts.

Did You Know?

The iconic GWK statue cost US$30 million and was 28 years in the making.

BALI'S SURF HISTORY

The 1960s saw the first surfers begin to arrive in Bali. They spoke of a "secret spot" on the southwestern tip – a place that would go on to become world-famous with the release of the 1971 surf movie *Morning of the Earth*. Meanwhile, a group of local Balinese youngsters broke through centuries-old beliefs that the sea was the home of demons. Using borrowed surfboards, they didn't take long to master the sport, although it would take them half a day to reach the spot where they thought the waves might be breaking. The lure of the surf has been deeply intertwined with the rise of tourism on Bali because the earliest guesthouses in Kuta were in fact built to accommodate visiting surfers.

13 🍴 ☕ 🛍️

Padang Padang Beach

🅐 D5 *i* Kuta; (0361) 754 092

Locally known as Pantai Labuan Sait, Padang Padang is an archetypically enchanting beach nestled into a pocket of lava rocks, complete with a long stretch of golden sand. Located on the northwestern coast of the Bukit Peninsula beside a road bridge over a river, it is accessed via a flight of stairs through a cave crevice. The surf has a steady set of barrels during good weather and is the venue for international surfing events, of which the Rip Curl Cup Padang Padang is the most frequently held. The beach was made famous by the Hollywood movie *Eat Pray Love* starring Julia Roberts and Javier Bardem. Jalan Labuan Sait, the road that loops past the beach, is lined with surf

camps, surf schools and surf shops, guesthouses, bungalow-style accommodation, cafés and local *warungs*, a boutique eco-resort and a five-star hotel. The whole area is characterized by a dry, rocky landscape dotted with stunted bush, cactus, kapok trees and wild flowers.

Pecatu

⚐D5 ℹ️Kuta; (0361) 754 092

Pecatu is the district that covers the southwest Bukit Peninsula, from Balangan Beach and Dreamland Beach on the peninsula's north coast, to Uluwatu at the western tip and Nyang Nyang Beach in the south. Until the turn of the 21st century, this dry-land outcrop was home solely to seaweed farmers, fishermen, cassava farmers and die-hard surfers. It is now the most upmarket destination on the island. The white-gold beaches here are among Bali's best, pounded by thrilling surf breaks. Party-goers will love the cliff-top Omnia Dayclub, and golfers will enjoy the 18-hole, championship-standard New Kuta Golf Course at Kawasan Pecatu Indah Resort, both of which command splendid ocean views.

Bingin Beach

⚐D4 ℹ️Kuta; (0361) 754 092

The white sand and pristine turquoise water of Bingin Beach is reached via a descent of hundreds of steep, crumbling steps, but you'll be rewarded with sensational views of the beautiful coastline and Indian Ocean as you zigzag past the rustic buildings that are set into the cliffs. When the tide is out, the beach is covered with fascinating rock pools. But when the tide is in, much of the beach vanishes, and you'll have to retreat to one of the many *warungs* that line the sand, from where you can watch Bingin's exceptional surf sets, rolling in, one after another. Close to the beach are plenty of homestays and cafés catering to the young surfing crowd.

← Tropical landscape of Bingin Beach, with a traditional Balinese-style hotel

---

TOP 5 EXPERIENCES ON THE BUKIT PENINSULA

Beer and Surf
Enjoy a Bintang beer at sunset at a cliff-top *warung* in Uluwatu (*p86*) while watching the fearless surfers performing their moves on the waves below.

Spa Relaxation
A two-hour session in the Thermes Marins Bali Aquatonic Pool at Ayana Resort & Spa (*www.ayana.com*) is an unforgettable journey through therapeutic jetstreams.

Fire Dance
Watch an exciting Kecak fire-dance performance at sunset at the cliff-top amphitheatre in the grounds of Uluwatu Temple (from 6pm daily; *p68*).

Hit the Clubs
Relax on the beach or party on the cliff top at one of the Bukit Peninsula's opulent beach clubs or day clubs.

Beach Trek
Get off the beaten track by descending 535 steps to the gorgeous, pristine white-sand Nyang Nyang Beach and relish the seclusion.

16 🍴 🍺 🏠

Uluwatu

🅰 D5

Bali's surf hotspot, Uluwatu is the most popular surf destination on the Bukit Peninsula due to its world-famous surf breaks. The area has many beach clubs and cliff-top day clubs with swimming pools, sunloungers and fine restaurants. Many cliff-top *warungs* offer views of the surf, cold beers and local dishes such as *nasi goreng* and fried noodles.

EAT & DRINK

Single Fin
With a huge balcony overlooking Uluwatu's surf break, this cliff-top surfer-friendly spot packs in the crowds and serves good pub grub.

🅰 D5 🏠 Pantai Suluban, Jalan Labuan Sait, Uluwatu
🌐 singlefinbali.com

Ⓡ Ⓡ Ⓡ

Bondi Grill'e
Plates of barbecued ribs, chicken, *mahi-mahi* and steak are served with chips or salad.

🅰 D5 🏠 Jalan Labuhan Sait, Uluwatu 📞 (0878) 6010 8053

Ⓡ Ⓡ Ⓡ

Delpi
Perched on a cliff, this café-bar offers superb views of the beach.

🅰 D5 🏠 Jalan Uluwatu, Pecatu 📞 (0878) 6001 6022

Ⓡ Ⓡ Ⓡ

Plentiful accommodation ranges from glamorous private estates, holiday villas and internationally branded boutique hotels to humble homestays. Despite its hipster vibe and a booming bar, café and restaurant culture, Uluwatu still retains a more laidback "Ulu" atmosphere than Kuta and Seminyak.

Access to Suluban Beach is via a steep concrete staircase through a narrow crag in a cliff. The beautiful beach is characterized by luminescent aquamarine water surrounded by limestone caves and cliffs. The best time to visit is during low tide, which reveals small caves and tidal pools that offer a pleasurable soak. Be sure to watch the tides, though, because the currents are strong, and waves can crash through cave openings. From here, surfers paddle out to the reef – this destination is for advanced or expert surfers only.

The area is also famous for the Pura Luhur Uluwatu temple (*p66*). Fascinating Kecak dance performances take place daily at 6pm at the open amphitheatre next to the temple against a glorious sunset.

↑ Surfers entering the waters at Uluwatu between the cliffs

17 🍴 🍺

Ungasan

🅰 E5

From Ungasan village's central position, 4 km (2.5 miles) from the Garuda Wisnu Kencana Cultural Park (*p83*) on the Bukit Peninsula, the Ungasan district extends to Bali's southernmost cliff, incorporating Karma Beach Club, Sunday's Beach Club, Banyan

→ Sun loungers and umbrellas at a luxury beach resort in Nusa Dua

Tree Resort, Melasti Beach and the isolated Green Bowl Beach. There is no coast road, so although these places are close to each other as the crow flies, they are a fair distance apart via narrow winding lanes. Green Bowl is reached via a 300-step descent. At low tide, the calm, clear waters allow for great snorkelling, while the surf waves are a short paddle beyond a natural reef barrier.

Nusa Dua

🅰 E4 🚍 ℹ Denpasar; (0361) 225 649

The Nusa Dua (literally "Two Islands") area is named after the two peninsulas along its coast. Built in the 1970s, the gated complex at Nusa Dua, for which the area is most famous, consists primarily of luxury resorts run by major hotel chains, and sandy beaches. The road leading to the entrance of the compound is lined with rows of statues; it leads through a large *candi bentar* (split gate), on each side of which carvings of frogs serve as guardian figures.

> **Suluban Beach is characterized by luminescent aquamarine water surrounded by limestone caves and cliffs. The best time to visit is during low tide.**

Inside is a calm atmosphere, away from the chaos of the rest of the island. The hotels are built on a big scale. Their grandiose entrances have been described as "Bali Baroque" or "expanded traditional" in style and are of interest to architecture enthusiasts. Young visitors will love the fish ponds of the Ayodya Resort, where thousands of brightly coloured *koi* (a type of carp first bred in Japan) swim among water lilies. The Bali National Golf Club has a championship course over three types of terrain (high-land, coconut grove and coastal). Regular dance and other cultural activities are held at Nusa Dua.

Other facilities include the Bali International Convention Centre, the Bali Collection Mall, restaurants and the large **Pasifika Museum** housing a collection of artworks, including paintings, sculpture and textiles, from Asian Pacific cultures spanning several centuries. There are also 20th-century paintings by European artists who lived in Bali, including Arie Smit, Adrien-Jean Le Mayeur and Theo Maier.

Outside the gates of the Nusa Dua complex is the bustling village of Bualu. Several streets are lined with restaurants offering fresh fish and shops selling handicrafts.

Between the Sheraton Laguna and Grand Hyatt hotels, a headland with native flora and several Balinese shrines juts out into the sea. The views from here are splendid. South of Geger Beach is a path that leads up to Pura Geger, a small temple.

West of Nusa Dua, on the road to Uluwatu, is the Garuda Wisnu Kencana Cultural Park (*p83*), which regularly stages exhibitions and performances.

Pasifika Museum
⊘ 🏠 Area Block P, Nusa Dua
🕐 10am–6pm daily
🌐 museum-pasifika.com

Stone arch and coral reef *(inset)* on the coast of Nusa Penida

19 🍴 🏬

Nusa Penida

🗺 F4 & G4 🚤 From Sanur, Kusamba & Padang Bai ⓘ Klungkung; (0366) 21 448

This quiet but developing island, once the penal colony of the Raja of Klungkung, is the legendary home of Ratu Gede Mecaling, the Balinese "King of Magical Powers". Here, Balinese language and art have been less subject to change than on the mainland. In general the landscape is dry, even arid, resembling the limestone hills of the Bukit Peninsula. Towards the south coast, with its tall white cliffs, there are a few lusher hills.

Reached via a 30-minute fastboat ride from Sanur, Nusa Penida is ripe for adventure and popular with day-trippers. There are no large resorts or fancy restaurants here but a fair number of homestays, budget hotels and quality *warungs*, most newly built on the north coast. The northeast coast is home to the gorgeous, remote Atuh Beach. Much of the west and south coast is only accessible via potholed roads, best carefully negotiated on a motorcycle. Nevertheless, a treasure chest of epic scenery awaits at Broken Beach, Angel's Billabong and Kelingking Beach, with its breathtaking vista of a golden-sand cove, reached via a perilous cliff-face descent.

Some cotton is grown on Nusa Penida. From it is woven the *cepuk*, a form of *ikat* textile (p136) thought to have magical, protective powers. Other local occupations include seaweed farming.

There are several interesting temples here. One is the Pura Ped, in the village of Toyapakeh. The temple is built on an island in a large lotus pond. Among the carvings in Pura Kuning, near Semaya, are some explicitly erotic reliefs. The *pura desa*, or village temple, of the inland village of Batumadeg also has some interesting decorative reliefs. They show sea creatures, including crabs and shellfish. The main gate is especially imposing.

On the southwest coast, Pura Gunung Cemeng is a temple balanced atop a pinnacle; from the neighbouring cliff tops, you can see graceful manta rays gliding through the waters 200 m (650 ft) below.

> 🔍 HIDDEN GEM
> ## Atuh Beach
>
> A blissful, hidden crescent of white sand, Atuh Beach is accessible via a steep stairway on one side or narrow tracks along a rugged cliff face on the other. It offers café shacks, sunbeds and umbrellas.

⑳ 🍴 🛍

Nusa Lembongan

🅐F4 🚤From Sanur, Kusamba & Padang Bai
ℹ️ Klungkung, Jalan Untung Surapati 3; (0366) 21 448

This small island has sandy beaches for sun-lovers and good coral reefs for divers and snorkellers. Bird-lovers will find a variety of species.

Day trips to the island have been available since the early 1990s. In operation now are several jet catamarans, the best known of them being the Bali Hai Cruises (www.balihaicruises.com); as a consequence the island is visited by larger groups than hitherto. Trips to the island are also offered by some local boat owners. The boats include *pinisi*, a type of Indonesian sailing vessel originating in the island of Sulawesi to the northeast.

Most boat operators rent watersports equipment, and snorkelling and diving gear.

On the island is an extensive underground house, known as the Cavehouse. It was dug by a Balinese priest after he was instructed in dreams to live in the belly of Mother Earth. He has passed away but the cave remains a popular curiosity.

For those who like pristine islands with no cars, Nusa Lembongan is a good place to stay a night or two. However, the best advice is to visit soon, because the island is developing quickly.

㉑

Nusa Ceningan

🅐F4

Linked to Nusa Lembongan by an iconic yellow suspension bridge, the tiny island of Nusa Ceningan is home to a small village of seaweed farmers. In the late afternoons you'll see their boats crowded around the plantations, reminiscent

A short distance south of Suana is a sacred limestone cave, Goa Karangsari.

Nusa Penida is also a haven for rare birds. Here, the Friends of the National Parks Foundation (FNPF) has been repopulating species since 2004. This and riches such as hidden bathing pools and virgin rainforest await the intrepid explorer.

The waters off the coast are crystal-clear, but the currents can be strong. Here experienced divers will spot many rare underwater species. There are fine coral formations, especially off the south coast, where the sea is famed for spectacular giant sunfish; these shy creatures, weighing up to 1,000 kg (2,200 lb), might be spied from July to October. Sailfish and the whale shark can also occasionally be seen. Off the northern half of the island the clear waters are shallower and calmer, especially in the strait between Nusa Penida and Nusa Lembongan. Most people who dive off these islands make their arrangements with operators in Sanur.

of a floating marketplace. Women are the main labourers; growth is fast and new shoots are harvested every 45 days. The produce is then dried and exported, mainly to Japan, for processing and use in cosmetics, food stabilizers and medicines. The natural sights of Ceningan are the stunning Blue Lagoon and Secret Beach, which is lapped by crystalline waters.

EAT

Tigerlillys
A tropical oasis, Tigerlillys offers breakfast, snacks and a lunch and dinner menu. Highlights include acai bowls and *san choy bau* (lettuce wraps).

🅐F4 🚪Jalan Jungutbatu, Jungutbatu, Nusa Lembongan 📞(0812) 4664 0343

Rp Rp Rp

Sandy Bay Beach Club
This beachside restaurant with a pool offers an all-day menu of Asian and international selections.

🅐F4 🚪Jalan Sandy Bay, Jungutbatu, Nusa Lembongan 🌐sandy baylembongan.com

Rp Rp Rp

Ogix Warung
Offering fabulous sea views from the cliffside, this open-air restaurant serves classic local dishes.

🅐F4 🚪Suana, Nusa Penida 📞(0813) 3937 7892

Rp Rp Rp

CENTRAL BALI

Central Bali's broad slopes, with their terraced rice fields and hundreds of villages, were the cradle of traditional Balinese society. This area encompasses the regency (and former kingdom) of Gianyar, made up of many *puri* (noble houses) whose former glory lives on in the courtly arts of sculpture, painting, gold- and silversmithing, music, dance and theatrical performance.

Between the Petanu and Pakrisan rivers are the remains of one of Bali's oldest civilizations. From the 9th to the 11th century, Bali was ruled by Hindu-Buddhist kingdoms centred near present-day Pejeng and Bedulu, a short distance from Ubud. After the Majapahit conquest in the 14th century, power shifted to Klungkung but it returned here in the 18th century. At that time branches of the Klungkung dynasty grew into rival kingdoms, two of which were based in Sukawati and Gianyar. Satellite *puri* competed in architectural and ritual display. Ubud became internationally famous as a gateway into Bali's cultural heartland when several Western artists and intellectuals settled here in the 1930s. As a major cultural and artistic centre, it still attracts many visitors today.

Pelaktiying

Telaga Waja

Sengkaduan

Bangkled

Kayuambua

Kerta

Tegal Suci

Tiga

Buahan
Kaja

Puakan

Tegalsuci

Kayang

Puhu

Carik

21 TARO

Tegal Payang

BANGLI

Ponggang

Puhu

Pura Tirta
Empul

Poyan

Pontang

20 SEBATU

Sulahan

Petang

Semaon

Tatag

Kebon

Gunung Kawi
Royal Monuments

Tegalsuci

Lebah

Perean Tengah

Payangan

Bukit

Getasan

22 TAMPAKSIRING

Bangli

TEGALLALANG 19

Padpadan

Demulih

Bebalang

Samuan

Kenderan

Sanding

Madangari

Kelabangmoding

Petak

Suwat

Gaga

NORTH AND
WEST BALI
p144

Junjungan

18 PETULU

Tarukan

Kabetan

Kedewatan

GIANYAR

Sangeh

16 AYUNG RIVER
GORGE

EAST BALI
p112

Selat

Sayan

2 UBUD

PEJENG

Bakbakan

Penestanan

15

Jagaperang

Dauh Yeh Cani

PELIATAN 14

13

11 BEDULU

Bunutin

GOA
GAJAH

Bitera

Sidan

Pengosekan

Kutri

Tusan

Kunba

9

Peteluan

Mambal

12

GIANYAR

Singapadu

MAS

Petanu

Tegal Tugu

Kaler

BLAHBATUH

10 BONA

Tulikup

Sedang

Sakah

17

8

Blega

Tedung

Lebih

BADUNG

KEMENUH

Medanan

BATUAN 6

Pering

Cucukan

7 SUKAWATI

BALI REPTILE PARK 4

Singapadu

Tebuana

Saba

BALI BIRD PARK 1

5

Rangkan

BATUBULAN 3

CELUK

Guwang

Kangin

Batuaji

Pabean

Ketewel

SOUTH BALI AND
THE BUKIT PENINSULA
p62

Gumicik

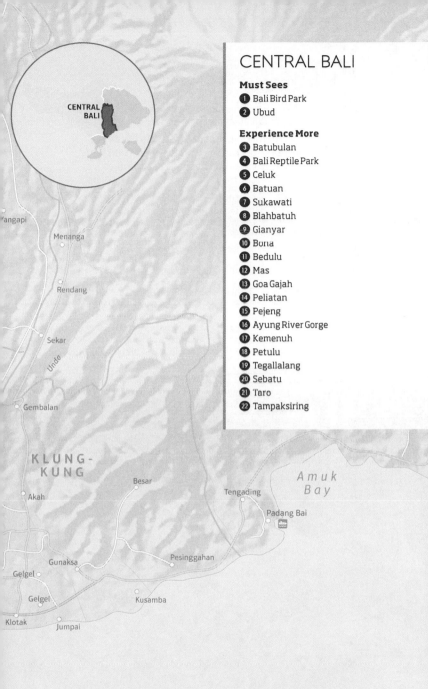

CENTRAL BALI

Must Sees
1. Bali Bird Park
2. Ubud

Experience More
3. Batubulan
4. Bali Reptile Park
5. Celuk
6. Batuan
7. Sukawati
8. Blahbatuh
9. Gianyar
10. Bona
11. Bedulu
12. Mas
13. Goa Gajah
14. Peliatan
15. Pejeng
16. Ayung River Gorge
17. Kemenuh
18. Petulu
19. Tegallalang
20. Sebatu
21. Taro
22. Tampaksiring

0 kilometres   3
0 miles   3

N

① 🦅 🎏 🍽 🖥 🛍

BALI BIRD PARK

🅰E4 🏠 Jalan Serma Cok Ngurah Gambir, Singapadu, Batubulan
🕘 9am–5:30pm daily 🌙 Nyepi 🌐 balibirdpark.com

Built on what was originally an expanse of rice fields, Bali Bird Park, or Taman Burung, is where visitors can see a profusion of exotic birds from Indonesia, Latin America, Africa and Australia at close quarters.

There are almost 1,000 birds here, many of them in big, walk-in aviaries. The park is committed to the preservation, conservation and breeding of many endangered species, including more than 40 species of Indonesian birds. The areas in which the birds are kept recreate their natural habitats, complete with indigenous plantlife, including more than 300 exotic trees and plants in a beautiful landscaped setting.

Bird Species

Among the 250 or so bird species in the Bird Park is the Australian Pelican, a large waterbird that sometimes wanders as far as Indonesia, and the lesser bird of paradise from New Guinea, which has been hunted close to extinction. You can also see the Victoria Crowned Pigeon, one of the three crowned pigeon species from New Guinea, the Nicorbar pigeon, the pink-necked pigeon, the great argus pheasant, the African Grey Parrot, which can be trained to mimic, and the Asian pied hornbill with its distinct, loud, raucous call.

Species being bred here include Bali's only endemic bird, the endangered Bali Starling *(Leucopsar rothschildi) (p148)*, as well as several species of parrots and coctakoos native to Indonesia and the attractive Australian Major Mitchell's cockatoo.

Scarlet Ibis, social and gregarious birds native to South America in the Bali Bird Park ↑

① Bali Starlings, Bali's only surviving indigenous bird.

② African crowned cranes.

③ Sun conures, vibrantly coloured parakeets native to South America.

OWL HOUSE

Rarely seen in the wild, Indonesian owls, such as the buffy fish owl and the barred or Sumatran eagle owl, are a highlight of the Bali Bird Park and are housed in the Toraja House, a typical house from Sulawesi. There are 38 recognized species of Indonesian owl. Their secretive nature and, in some cases, inhospitable habitats, are reasons why little is known about them.

← Buffy fish owl, which lives near water and eats fish

Did You Know?

Free-flight shows take place at 10:30am and 4:30pm daily.

↑ Pura Taman Saraswati, with a pond full of beautiful lotus blossoms

2 🍴 🖥 🛍

UBUD

🅐 E3 🚌 from Denpasar & Kuta ℹ️ Jalan Raya Ubud; (0361) 973 285

Bali's cultural and artistic heart, Ubud is packed with galleries, art studios, museums and shops selling handicrafts, woodcarvings, jewellery, paintings and textiles, as well as restaurants and cafés. The town's artistic traditions can be seen everywhere.

① Pura Taman Saraswati

🅐 Jalan Kajen, off Jalan Raya Ubud 🕐 Daily

This temple was built in the 1950s by the Balinese stone sculptor and architect I Gusti Nyoman Lempad at the command of Ubud's prince, in honour of Saraswati, the Hindu deity of learning and the arts. A fine example of classical Balinese temple architecture, it is set in a water garden, with a lotus pond as the centrepiece. The temple has fine carvings by Lempad: a 3-m (10-ft) statue of the demon Jero Gede Mecaling; and the *padmasana* shrine in the northeast corner, dedicated to the Supreme God.

② Puri Saren

🅐 Jalan Raya Ubud 📞 (0361) 975 057 🕐 Daily

The grandeur of Puri Saren, Ubud's royal palace, dates from the 1890s, the time of warlord Cokorda Gede Sukawati. The present walls, resplendent gates and stone carvings are largely the work of master artist I Gusti Nyoman Lempad. The traditional buildings are set in a charming garden.

The *puri* (local royal family) still lives here. It remains influential in Ubud's religious and cultural life and spends lavishly on local ceremonies. Nightly traditional dance performances take place at the palace at 7:30pm.

③ Lempad House

🅐 Jalan Raya Ubud 📞 (0361) 975 618 🕐 Daily

This is the family home of I Gusti Nyoman Lempad (1862–1978), perhaps Bali's most celebrated artist. Some sculptures by Lempad are on display in the beautiful Balinese garden and a small collection of his line drawings and paintings can be seen inside the house. The Neka Art Museum *(p98)* holds a larger collection of his work.

Lempad was also an architect and builder in the traditional Balinese style, and the handsome north and east

💬 INSIDER TIP
Tourist Information

The Tourist Information Centre on Jalan Rayan Ubud provides excellent information about guided tours, transport, dance performances and other cultural events in Ubud. It also advises on dress etiquette when visiting temples or traditional religious ceremonies.

pavilions of the house were designed by him. He was the architect of many of the palaces and temples throughout Ubud. As a painter, his line drawings, which drew inspiration from local folklore, were very influential in the Balinese art scene.

④ 🏛 Ubud Market

📍 Jalan Raya Ubud, opposite Puri Saren Palace
🕐 Daily

Ubud's huge, busy market is where the Balinese do their shopping early each morning before much of the fresh produce is whisked away to make room for more tourist-oriented handicrafts. Spices, fruits, vegetables, hardware, textiles and woven baskets are all available amid the chaos of the heaped stalls. Everything sold here is grown, crafted, or produced in Bali. If you're more interested in purchasing souvenirs or artwork, visit the market later in the day and you'll find stalls specializing in woodcarvings, wind-chimes, paintings, bags, quilts, sarongs, silk scarves, traditional textiles such as *ikat*, and all manner of handicrafts including lamps, coasters and wooden trays. All of these are handmade in the surrounding craft villages. Bargaining is essential.

⑤ 💻 Pondok Pekak Library and Learning Center

📍 East side of the football field, Monkey Forest Rd
🕐 9am–5pm Mon–Sat, 1–5pm Sun 🌐 pondok pekaklibrary.com

The library here has more than 30,000 books, including bestsellers, philosophy titles, memoirs and children's books, many in English. Dedicated to preserving

Bali's traditional culture and art practices, the superb, friendly learning centre offers visitors fun classes in traditional Balinese dance, *gamelan* music, making Balinese offerings, fruit carving, cooking, silver jewellery making, painting, wood-carving, mask-making and many other crafts. This is a great place for families, as many of the classes are geared towards children.

↑ Stalls displaying an array of brightly coloured handicrafts at Ubud Market

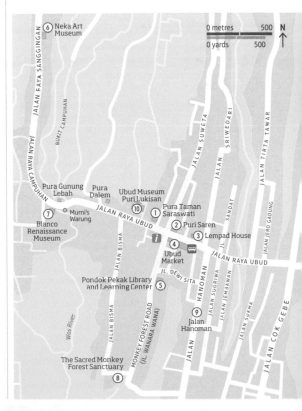

⑥ ⚎

Neka Art Museum

🏠 Jalan Raya Sanggingan, Campuhan ⏰ 9am-5pm Mon-Sat, noon-5pm Sun 🌐 museumneka.com

Founded in 1976 by art connoisseur Suteja Neka, the museum consists of a series of pavilions presenting an overview of the different historical styles of Balinese painting. This ranges from classical narrative Wayan painting and the Ubud and Batuan styles to contemporary works. The Arie Smit Pavilion is devoted to this Dutch-born artist, while the East-West Annexe showcases other foreign artists, including Miguel Covarrubias, Rudolf Bonnet, Han Snel and Donald Friend. You can also see black-and-white photographs of Bali during the 1930s and early '40s by Robert Koke, and Bali's largest collections of art by I Gusti Nyoman Lempad.

↑ Stone figure holding a *keris* (traditional dagger), Neka Art Museum

---

EAT

Murni's Warung
Ubud's first real restaurant, created in 1974 by Ibu Murni, who still owns and runs it, is famous not only for its excellent local food dishes but also for its art displays.

🏠 Jalan Raya Campuan, Ubud 🌐 murnis.com

Rp Rp Rp

---

⑦ ⚎

Blanco Renaissance Museum

🏠 Jalan Raya Campuhan, Campuhan Bridge ⏰ 9am-5pm daily 🌐 blancomuseum.com

The late Spanish artist Antonio Blanco (1912–99), captivated by Bali, built this palatial house and studio at the top of a steep driveway in Ubud next to Campuhan Bridge in the 1950s. The flamboyant Blanco is best known for his romantic, idealised paintings, collages, illustrated poetry and lithographic artworks, whose main subjects were women. Among his models were his Balinese wife – the celebrated dancer Ni Ronji – and their daughter.

The main gallery is a massive, sumptuous hall with marble floors, huge pillars and a domed roof. The colourful walls are lined with about 300 of Blanco's artworks in lavish and unusual frames displayed in chronological order, as well as some paintings by his son, Mario. The beautiful, cascading gardens house a waterfall, friendly parrots and other exotic birds and offer good views over the river.

Did You Know?

Showing your teeth can be interpreted as a sign of aggression by macaques.

---

⑧ ⚎

The Sacred Monkey Forest Sanctuary

🏠 Jalan Monkey Forest, Padangtegal ⏰ 8:30am-6pm daily 🌐 monkeyforestubud.com

Ubud's Monkey Forest jungle offers protection to more than 600 long-tailed Balinese macaques, which are fascinating to observe, especially with their young. Follow the paved pathways through the forest and be sure to conceal your camera and other shiny objects, as the mischievous macaques may snatch them and run off in a flash (if this happens, ask the staff for assistance).

There are also three temples here, founded in the 14th century. The largest is the Pura

↑ Macaques on a flight of steps in the Sacred Monkey Forest Sanctuary

Dalem Agung (Great Temple of the Dead), with its ornately carved gate located at the highest point of the forest. A long flight of steps and a bridge over a river leads to the Holy Bathing Temple, while the third temple, the Pura Prajapati funeral temple, is situated next to one of two graveyards in the forest. Despite its small size, the forest has around 115 different species of trees.

⑨ 🍴 🍹 🏠

Jalan Hanoman

Running parallel to Monkey Forest Road, Jalan Hanoman is lined on both sides with small, glass-fronted shops selling homewares, jewellery, clothing and art. Catering to Ubud's thriving community of spiritual seekers, many of the clothing stores sell yoga gear and accessories ranging from intricately designed Himalayan *cakra* and *mandala* paintings, Tibetan singing bowls, crystals and meditational beads to musical instruments to accompany chanting meditations, aromatic incenses and burning oils. The street is also home to a wide selection of restaurants and small cafés, many of which are vegetarian. Hanoman is the monkey god and his image can be seen at temples along the street.

INFLUENTIAL VISITORS OF THE 1930S

Bali owes much of its fame to foreign guests of Ubud's royal family in the 1920s and 1930s. Through their films, books and photographs, these visitors projected to the world an exotic image of Bali. Among the most influential were German painter and musician Walter Spies *(right)*, Dutch painter Rudolf Bonnet and Mexican artist Miguel Covarrubias, who wrote the classic *Island of Bali* (1937). American and English anthropologists Margaret Mead and Gregory Bateson lived in Sayan, just outside Ubud; their neighbours were Canadian composer Colin McPhee and his American wife, ethnographer Jane Belo.

⑩ 🖐 🎭 🍴 🖼 🛍

UBUD MUSEUM PURI LUKISAN

🏠 Jalan Raya Ubud 🕐 9am–6pm daily 🚫 Public hols
🌐 museumpurilukisan.com

With superb examples of all schools of modern Balinese art, Museum Puri Lukisan ("Palace of Painting") has a large collection of paintings and wood-carvings and is one of the leading art galleries and museums in Bali.

The brainchild of Ubud's prince Cokorda Gede Agung Sukawati and Dutch painter Rudolf Bonnet, the museum was conceived in 1953 out of concern that Bali's finest works of art were disappearing into private collections around the world. Its holdings are mainly 20th-century Balinese painting and wood sculpture, including the colourful paintings of the Batuan School, the highly stylised art of Sanur and the intricately detailed pieces of the Ubud style, with a focus on the 1930s.

LOOKING AT BALINESE PAINTINGS

The density of Balinese painting is extraordinary. Even with little or no background in the arts, the viewer can enter the imaginative world of Balinese culture as represented by both traditional and modern painting. It is a good idea to look at a Balinese work from a distance at first, to see its graphic composition before moving nearer to inspect the details of the content. Close inspection reveals tiny scenes being enacted by the inhabitants of the canvas, a bit like a comic strip.

←

Dewi Sri (1960), rice goddess with a grain of rice in her hand, by Ketut Djedeng

↑ Main entrance gate to the Museum Puri Lukisan, set in gardens with ponds; gallery in the museum displaying modern Balinese art *(inset)*

EXPERIENCE MORE

3

Batubulan

A E4 **🚌** **ℹ** Ubud; (0361) 973 285

Although Denpasar's urban sprawl is enveloping Batubulan and the main road is lined with shops selling "antique" furniture, this large village is still a centre of traditional stone carving. Craftsmen can be seen in countless workshops sculpting mytho-logical and religious figures or highly imaginative modern forms, apparently oblivious to the heavy traffic passing by.

The village temple, **Pura Puseh** (entry with donation), is a good example of the use of *paras*, Bali's ubiquitous grey stone, which is in fact volcanic tuff, quarried from river gorges. *Paras* is used both for sculpture and as a building material. Its soft texture makes it easy to carve.

Batubulan is also home to several venerable Barong and *keris* dance theatre troupes. During alternate weeks the Pura Puseh hosts a daily performance (starting at 9:30am) by the celebrated Denjalan troupe; in intervening weeks the venue is Batubulan's *bale banjar*, or community pavilion. Other troupes may also take part. These daytime performances began in the 1930s, so that visitors might take photographs. However, this exorcistic drama still has ritual significance.

Pura Puseh
🏠 Main Road, Batubulan
🕐 Daily

4

Bali Reptile Park

A E3 **🏠** Jalan Serma Cok Ngurah Gambir, Singapadu (next to Bali Bird Park) **📞** (0361) 299 352 **🕐** Daily **✖** Nyepi

The Bali Reptile Park (Rimba Reptil) can be visited together with the Bali Bird Park *(p94)* next door, on the same entrance ticket. Although somewhat smaller than the Bird Park, the Reptile Park is also set in lush, botanically interesting gardens. The landscaping concept is that of an ancient archaeological site, excavated and restored to its former glory. Among the native Indonesian species are Komodo dragons, four species of crocodiles, and possibly the largest known python in captivity. Venomous snakes from around the world, well displayed in glass cages, include a king cobra, a Malayan pit viper and a death adder.

5

Celuk

A E3 **🚌** **ℹ** Ubud; (0361) 973 285

The village of Celuk is devoted almost entirely to gold- and silversmithing. Much of the jewellery sold in Bali originates here. The workers belong to the caste clan of Pande Mas, traditionally practitioners of various metal crafts. Grand jewellery shops line the main road; smaller ones selling cheaper goods occupy the

Batubulan's Pura Puseh, a venue for traditional Barong and *keris* dance performances ↑

BALINESE SILVER JEWELLERY

Using the most basic of tools, Balinese silversmiths handcraft intricate designs from sterling silver, enhanced by a technique called granulation, where small pellets and tiny coiled silver wires are heated until soft enough to adhere to the piece to form a pattern or decorative feature. These miniature works of art are then set with precious and semi-precious gemstones. Styles are distinctive and constantly replicated.

narrow side streets. Several studios make traditional and modern jewellery designs to order, as well as *kcris* daggers and religious items. Be aware that at larger outlets, prices may include a fat commission passed on to tour guides.

Batuan

E3 🚌 *i* Ubud; (0361) 973285

Batuan, an ancient settlement whose population contains more nobility than commoners, is celebrated for its artistic excellence not only in the field of dance but also in painting and architecture. Painters' studios abound in the village. The Batuan school of painting is known for its dense graphics, dramatically restricted colour palette and astute observation of human life.

The Pura Puseh, the magnificent village temple, welcomes visitors. Extensively renovated, its opulent shrines and carvings are proof that Bali's traditional building arts are thriving. *Gambuh* performances are held at the temple at 7pm on the 1st and 15th of each month, a rare opportunity to see this ancient court dance.

Sukawati

E3 🚌 *i* Ubud; (0361) 973285

Sukawati is worth visiting primarily as a handicrafts centre. Opposite the farmers' market on the east side of the main road is the Pasar Seni ("Art Market"): a complex of two-storey buildings packed with craft stalls. Behind it is a market selling woodcarvings, open until 7pm daily.

To the people of Bali, Sukawati is important as the ancestral seat of many of the region's *puri* (noble houses), and as a centre of the sacred shadow puppet theatre, *wayang kulit*. In the early 1700s an offshoot of the royal house of Klungkung was established here, but its palace is now greatly reduced and the temples are not generally open to visitors.

Blahbatuh

E3 🚌 *i* Ubud; (0361) 973285

The village of Blahbatuh is marked by a huge stone statue of a baby, erected in the early 1990s. It is said by some to be the village giant Kebo Iwo as an infant; others whisper that the women of a nearby village urged their husbands to build the statue to placate a demon who they believed had been claiming the lives of their children.

Vihara Amurva Bhumi Blahbatuh, a Chinese temple *(klenteng)* with Buddhist and Hindu elements which has expanded in grand style, is an increasingly popular centre of worship for Chinese Buddhists from throughout South Bali.

Outside the village on the Bedulu road is the large workshop and showroom of the **Sidha Karya Gong Foundry**, established by the renowned gongsmith I Made Gabeleran. A full array of traditional musical instruments and dance costumes is on sale.

At Kutri, 3 km (2 miles) north of Blahbatuh, is a hill at the base of which is the Pura Bukit Dharma Kutri temple complex. On the hilltop, from which there are good views, is a shrine that houses a partly effaced, but still fine, relief carving of the goddess Durga killing a bull. It is thought to be based on an 11th-century Balinese queen.

Sidha Karya Gong Foundry
🏠 Jalan Raya Getas-Buruan, Blahbatuh 📞 (0361) 942798

> Batubulan craftsmen can be seen in countless workshops sculpting mythological and religious figures or highly imaginative modern forms.

←
Baskets of fresh local produce at the central market in Gianyar

Sanghyang dance, which could only be staged in the temple. Then, in the early 1930s, artists from Bona developed a fire dance using the story of Ramayana as a substitute for the Sanghyang dance so that it could be performed in public.

9

Gianyar

Ⓐ E3 🚌 **ⓘ Ubud; (0361) 973 285**

This town is a centre of administration rather than of the tourist industry. The people of Bali shop here for farm produce, household appliances and paraphernalia for ceremonies; there is also a large night market. This is a good place to buy jewellery and hand-woven and hand-dyed textiles, many of them made locally. However, it is particularly popular for its food stalls, which cook a range of delicious dishes; the *babi guling* (roast pig) is famous.

STAY

Komune Resort

A remote black-sand beach is home to this 66-room retreat and beach club, with organic restaurant, spa and pool. The theme here is surfing, yoga and wellness.

Ⓐ E3 **Ⓐ Jalan Pantai Keramas, Medahan, Blahbatuh**
ⓦ komuneresorts.com

Ⓡⓟ Ⓡⓟ Ⓡⓟ

On the north side of the town square is the impressive Puri Gianyar. Although the palace is closed to visitors, its grand outer walls and gates give a sense of the power of the former kingdoms. After damage by an earthquake in 1917, the *puri* was restored as a replica of the original 17th-century construction.

---

10 🏛️

Bona

Ⓐ E3 Ⓐ Between Blahbatuh and Gianyar

Southwest of Gianyar, several villages increasingly make their livelihood by crafting products from native plant materials. Although these are sold for export and in shops around Bali, tourists can buy them for much better prices at source. The village of Bona specializes in making bamboo furniture. However, the attractive items hand-woven by the artisans here from dried lontar fan-palm leaves are perhaps more practicable purchases for the visitor. The variety is enormous and the quality is good; as well as baskets, hats, sandals, wallets and fans there are also dolls, birds, flowers and even Christmas trees.

Bona is also the place where the dramatic modern Kecak dance was born. Kecak was originally the music that accompanied the sacred

11

Bedulu

Ⓐ E3 🚌 **ⓘ Ubud; (0361) 973 285**

This large, quiet village was at the centre of the Pejeng kingdom of the 10–13th centuries. The monumental relief carvings on a large rock wall at the **Yeh Pulu** spring, south of the village, are thought to date from the mid-14th-century Majapahit conquest (*p54*). The carvings – about 25 m (80 ft) long with an average height of 2 m (6 ft) – are thought to be the work of a single artist. Myth attributes the work to the legendary 14th-century giant Kebo Iwo. The stories can be "read" from left to right. Among them are shadow puppet characters, Hindu gods and ordinary people. Heroic scenes show humans fighting demonic beasts.

The large Pura Pengastulan temple has grand gates built in the Art Deco style made fashionable by the artist I Gusti Nyoman Lempad, who was born in Bedulu. Lempad's style may be seen also in the inner gate at the nearby **Pura Samuan Tiga** (entry with donation). Its name derives from a legend: in the 11th century, a meeting (*samuan*) is said to have been held here among the gods of three (*tiga*) warring religious sects after they had defeated the demon king Mayadanawa.

THE LEGEND OF BEDULU

Bedulu (or Bedaulu) was a 14th-century sorcerer-king who was said to remove his head *(hulu)* in order to meditate more effectively. One day he was disturbed in this practice and hastily put the head of a pig back onto his shoulders. Thereafter it was forbidden to look at the king, lest his ugly secret be discovered, and he ruled from a tower, raised above eye level. However, the Majapahit general Gajah Mada tricked him during a feast. As Gajah Mada tipped back his head to drink, he looked up, glimpsed the king's pig's head and so was able to overpower him.

Even when empty, this temple has a great, quiet strength, but it bursts into life during the annual festival on the full moon of the twelfth month in a brilliant 11-day celebration. Don't miss the Perang Sampian warrior ceremony at lunchtime: a graceful procession by white-clad women followed by rowdy mock-fighting among crowds of young men brandishing elaborate palm-leaf whisks.

Yeh Pulu
◈ ⏰ Daily

Pura Samuan Tiga
⏰ Daily

---

⑫ 🍴 💻 🛍️

Mas

🅰 E3 🚌 ℹ️ Gianyar; (0361) 973 285

The village of Mas is most famous not for teak furniture, as the number of roadside shops selling it might suggest, but for fine wood sculpture and *topeng* masks used in theatre performances. The Brahmans of Mas have been master-carvers for many generations, producing sculpture for the art market since the 1930s. Among the best-established studio-galleries are Siadja & Son, the Njana Tilem Gallery and Adil Artshop. Tantra Gallery and I B Anom (for masks) are also well known. Brahmans come to Mas from all over Bali during every Galungan festival *(p52)* to honour their ancestor, the Hindu priest Dang Hyang Nirartha (also known as Dwijendra) at the Pura Taman Pule. The large old tree in this temple is regarded as holy. According to local belief, a gold flower once grew from it. On the evening of the festivities there is usually a ritual performance of *wayang wong* (where characters wear masks and move like puppets).

↑ Carved water buffalo skull, an example of Mas craftsmanship

↑ The Yeh Pulu rock carvings south of Bedulu village

13

Goa Gajah

E3 Ubud; (0361) 973 285 Daily

The Goa Gajah ("Elephant Cave") became known to Westerners only in 1923. It is thought to date from the 11th century. Steps lead down to the temple and other monuments, about 15 m (50 ft) below road level. The large springs, excavated in 1954, were probably intended for bathing and as a source of holy water. The cave itself, with a large face exuberantly carved in the surrounding rock, is a small, rather airless, T-shaped chamber in which are niches containing Shivite and Buddhist statues.

Outside the cave is a shrine to the Buddhist child-protector Hariti, depicted as the Balinese Men Brayut, a poor woman with too many children. In a ravine a little to the south is a spring and more shrines.

14

Peliatan

E3 From Ubud
Ubud; (0361) 973 285

The village of Peliatan, once the seat of an offshoot of the royalty of Sukawati, has long been renowned for its artistic traditions. Today, Peliatan's gamelan and dance troupes travel abroad as cultural ambassadors, as well as performing locally.

Peliatan is also a centre of painting and woodcarving. Many artists' studios can be found along its main street and back lanes. The collector Agung Rai established the successful Agung Rai Gallery and the impressive **Agung Rai Museum of Art** (ARMA). Its collections include classical Kamasan paintings on tree bark, works by Batuan artists from the 1930s, pieces by Javanese and Balinese masters and paintings by Walter Spies, Lempad, Bonnet and Le Mayeur. There are also contemporary Balinese and Indonesian works. The museum offers classes in painting and gamelan and many other cultural courses.

Also of note is the **Rudana Museum**, which houses traditional paintings by Balinese artists, as well as some modern works.

The northern part of Peliatan, known as Andong, has some interesting craft shops.

Agung Rai Museum of Art
Jalan Pengosekan
Daily armabali.com

Rudana Museum
Jalan Cok Rai Pudak 44
(0361) 975 779 Daily

← Jungle stairway *(below)* leading to Goa Gajah cave entrance *(left)*

15

Pejeng

E3 From Ubud & Gianyar Ubud; (0361) 973 285

Pejeng, a village on the road from Bedulu to Tampaksiring, lies at the heart of the ancient Pejeng-Bedulu kingdom, and there are many interesting relics from that time to be seen. The **Museum Purbakala** (Archaeological Museum) (entry with donation) displays

Artist painting at the Agung Rai Museum of Art (ARMA), Peliatan ↑

> **The Agung Rai Museum of Art offers classes in painting and gamelan and many other cultural courses.**

fascinating prehistoric objects in bronze, stone and ceramics, including several turtle-shaped stone sarcophagi.

Nearby are three temples of particular interest for their sacred stone sculptures. Just across the road from the museum, Pura Arjuna Metapa (Arjuna Meditating Temple) is a small pavilion standing alone in the rice fields, sheltering a cluster of stone sculptures that were probably once part of a spring temple. In accordance with the *wayang* tradition that recounts tales from the *Mahabharata*, Arjuna is attended by a stone-relief servant character.

About 100 m (110 yards) north is Pura Kebo Edan (Crazy Giant Temple), whose demonic statuary suggests that this was a cult-temple of Bhairava Buddhism. The chief figure is a masked 3.6 m- (12 ft-) high giant, dancing on a corpse. At the beautifully proportioned Pura Pusering Jagat (Navel of the World Temple), numerous pavilions house similar Tantric stone figures. The Pejeng Vessel, a cylindrical stone urn carved with cosmological figures, is kept in a shrine in the southeastern corner of the temple.

About 2 km (1 mile) north of Pejeng, Pura Penataran Sasih houses the Pejeng Moon (*sasih* means moon), a bronze drum 186 cm (74 inches) long, of unknown age. Considered sacred, it is kept in a tall pavilion. Temple guides sometimes allow visitors to stand on the base of an adjacent shrine; from here, you can glimpse the drum's fine geometric patterning. The design is associated with the Dong-son culture of southern China and northern Vietnam of around 1500 BC.

Museum Purbakala
🏠 Pejeng 📞 (0361) 942 347
🕑 8am–4pm Mon–Fri

🔢 16 🍴 🏛

Ayung River Gorge

🅰 E3 🚌 From Ubud
ℹ Ubud; (0361) 973 285

Between Kedewatan and Sayan, the east bank of the spectacularly beautiful Ayung River Gorge is discreetly populated with luxury hotels and private houses. Several companies offer white-water rafting from points on both sides of the river.

In the village of Penestanan, just east of the gorge, there are studios producing painted batik and beadwork. This is also the centre of the Young Artists movement, which emerged in the 1960s. Influenced by Dutch artist Arie Smit, who lived in Penestanan, these artists produced paintings in very bright, vivid colours.

> ## WOODCARVING IN BALI
>
> The surprising abundance of Balinese woodcarving reflects not only an intense decorative tradition but also the fact that Bali's wilderness is forest. Trees have a ritual anniversary and must be given offerings before being felled. Traditional woodcarving is of two main sorts: ritual objects such as effigies and masks; and ornamental carving, especially of architectural elements. The liberalizing art movement of the 1930s encouraged woodcarvers to sculpt freely for a foreign market. The main centres of woodcarving today include Peliatan and several other villages in Gianyar regency, including Tegallalang *(p108)* and Mas *(p105)*.

←
Emerald-green bathing pool at the stunning Tegenungan Waterfall

viewing spot is the road from the Junungan direction through the rice fields.

It is not known why the birds suddenly settled in Petulu in 1965. According to local legend, they are the souls of the estimated 500,000 Balinese people killed during the anti-Communist massacres of 1965–6.

⑰ Kemenuh
🅰E3 🚶9 km (6 miles) south of Ubud

The village of Kemenuh has a long-standing woodcarving tradition. Workshops and galleries selling wooden sculptures of animals and mythological figures can be found throughout the village.

Two trekking trails lead from the village through the spectacular scenery of the Petani River Valley. The main attraction here is the 20 m (65 ft) high **Tegenungan Waterfall**, which is framed by dense foliage and accessed down a stairway of 172 steps. At the vast pebbly base of the falls, you can enjoy a dip in the plunge pool, and there are several cafés nearby.

Tegenungan Waterfall
⊛ 🄰 Jalan Raya Tegenungan, Kemenuh, Sukawati 🄾Dawn-dusk

⑱ Petulu
🅰E3 🚌From Ubud & Pujung 🄸Ubud; (0361) 973 285

In the late afternoon every day, a remarkable, natural phenomenon occurs in the tiny village of Petulu as

thousands of white *kokokan* (egrets and pond herons) fly in to roost for the night. The huge flocks of birds arrive in a steady throng, filling the sky, wheeling and finally landing in the tall palms and old fig trees, where they squabble over prime perches. Village tradition dictates that the herons, which are considered sacred, may not be disturbed while they roost.

The V-formations of birds against the background of the sunset form an unforgettable sight. Visitors are welcome to watch them from the upper floor of the village community building. Another good

⑲ 🍴 ◻ 🛍

Tegallalang
🅰E3 🚌From Ubud 🄸Ubud; (0361) 973 285

The captivating village of Tegallalang, once the seat of a kingdom, is interesting as a centre of the wood-carving industry. Workshops and simple wholesale outlets line the road for some 5 km (3 miles), selling a variety of wooden handicrafts at very low prices. There are several small cafés along the main road that overlook the truly spectacular, lush rice

→
The beautiful, much-photographed Tegallalang rice terraces

Did You Know?

The Tegallalang rice terraces use traditional irrigation techniques from the 9th century.

terraces sculpted into the side of the river gorge north of Tegallalang.

Not far from here, Kebon is a pretty village reached by a steep side road 3 km (2 miles) north of Tegallalang. At the junction with the main road is the excellent Kampung Cafe, a restaurant with several suites of accommodation. Kenderan, also on a back road, is a former micro-kingdom with several small *puri* (houses of the nobility).

The village of Manuaba, about 4 km (2 miles) north of Kenderan, is notable for its Brahman temple **Pura Griya Sakti**, with its refurbished *wantilan* performance pavilion. A visit to see the huge intertwined trees behind the inner courtyard requires permission of the temple attendant.

There is an interesting holy spring, Telaga Waja, in Kapitu, 1 km (half a mile) south of Kenderan. Access is by way of a 200-m (220-yard) footpath and a long, steep flight of steps. There are traces of meditation niches which suggest that Telaga Waja was once a Buddhist retreat, possibly over 1,000 years ago.

Pura Griya Sakti
◈ △ Manuaba ⏲ Daily

___

20 🍴 🍽
Sebatu

🅰 E2 🚌 From Ubud
🛈 Ubud; (0361) 973 285

Sebatu village, part of a larger area of the same name, is highly regarded among the Balinese not only for its painted wood sculpture but also for its dance, music and classical dance costumes. Easily explored on foot, the village is laid out on a grid of three north–south streets, with the temples and *bale banjar* (community pavilion) at the northern end. The western-most street is lined with studios making woodcarvings that are offered for sale to visitors.

In a little valley on the western outskirts of Sebatu itself is the lovely spring temple **Pura Gunung Kawi**, not to be confused with the royal monuments of the same name near Tampaksiring *(p110)*. The bathing pools, fed via carved stone waterspouts, are worth seeing (but should not be photographed if they are in use), as is the carp-filled spring pool in the northwest corner. In the centre of the pool is a handsome shrine. There are several interesting sculptures among the small, colourfully painted pavilions in the central courtyard.

Pura Gunung Kawi
◈ ⏲ Daily

___

📷 PICTURE PERFECT
Lose the Crowds

So beautiful are the rice terraces of Tegallalang that the road above is firmly on the tourist photo-op circuit. For some different, more immersive viewpoints, ask one of the locals for a guided visit into the fields. A small fee is expected.

Did You Know?

A glowing tree is said to have shown Rsi Markandya where to found Taro - derived from *taru*, "tree".

21

Taro

E2 *Ubud; (0361) 973 285*

Taro is said to be one of the very earliest settlements in Bali. At the village centre is the large Pura Gunung Raung temple. Looking over its walls it is possible to admire the long *bale agung* pavilion, and a glowering three-tier *meru* pagoda. The latter represents the East Javanese mountain Gunung Raung, from where the legendary sage Rsi Markandya and his followers set out in the 8th century on a mission to Bali that ended here.

Taro is the source of Bali's albino cattle, valued for their importance in large rituals. Formerly they were sacrificed; today they are merely lent out for the ceremony and then returned. The herd wanders freely in the forest south of the village.

Also in Taro is the Elephant Safari Park, which allows visitors to interact with and learn about Sumatran elephants. There's also a museum of elephants and their history, a large restaurant and a spa hotel.

22

Tampaksiring

E3 *From Bedulu & Gianyar* *Ubud; (0361) 973 285*

Tampaksiring is most famously the site of the 10th-century water temple of **Tirta Empul**.

Here, clear freshwater springs, said possess magical curative powers, bubble up within the temple and gush out through spouts into an elaborately carved bathing pool. Locals flock to this holy place in search of blessings and cleansing rituals.

Nearby is **Gunung Kawi**, approached via a steep descent flanked by rice fields. This is the site of ten ancient royal shrines dedicated to 11th-century Balinese royalty, carved out of the rock face of the Pakerisan River Gorge.

Tampaksiring is also home to the serene, picturesque **Pura Mengening** water temple, where a holy spring emanates from under a banyan tree.

North of Tirta Empul is the Presidential Palace, an opulent hilltop retreat built in the 1950s for Indonesia's first president, the half-Balinese Sukarno. It overlooks Tirta Empul and the story goes that the dictator would spy through a telescope on the naked women bathing below. Visitors wishing to enter the palace must apply in writing to the Presidential Office in Tampaksiring, and a formal dress code is applied.

Tirta Empul
⊗ ⌂ Jalan Tirta, Manukaya
🕐 7am-6pm daily

Gunung Kawi
⊗ ⌂ Banjar Penaka
🕐 7am-6 pm daily

Pura Mengening
⊗ ⌂ Jalan Tirta, Sareseda
🕐 7am-6pm daily

PRESIDENTIAL PHANTOM

Don't be surprised if you feel a shiver down your spine at the Presidential Palace at Tampaksiring. President Sukarno died in 1970, but local legend has it that his ghost still roams the palace.

↑ Royal memorial tombs carved from the rock face at Gunung Kawi, Tampaksiring

Rays of light in the morning mist in the Sidemen Valley

EAST BALI

The three regencies of Klungkung, Bangli and Karangasem comprise the East Bali area. Some of the island's most important temples and palaces are in this region. A tradition of royal grandeur dates back to the 15th century, when the court of the first king of Gelgel was established. What remains of the palaces and temples is a window into a world of ceremony and tradition, focused around Gunung Agung, centre of the Balinese universe. Around the courts and palaces the arts flourished and villages of skilled artisans grew up. This tradition of craftsmanship survives in many places today.

In the 14th century the Javanese kingdom of Majapahit brought to Bali a new social order and caste system. Some communities resisted it, and their descendants, known as the Bali Aga (original Balinese), still live here in culturally distinct villages such as Tenganan and Trunyan.

Klungkung's royal house came to an end in 1908, when the king and members of his court committed *puputan (p55)*, rather than submit to Dutch colonial control. However, many architectural relics remain as reminders of pre-colonial times.

The region was devastated by Mount Agung's eruption in 1963 and by an earthquake in 1976; in many places great lava flows transformed the landscape.

PACUNG
BONDALEM
Tedjakula

BULELENG

Madenan   Geretek

Satra   Lupak
                                                   Kertabuana
Dausa   Tianyar
Bantang   Sukawana
    20 PURA TEGEH KORIPAN   Karansari
        Penulisan   Nusu
                              Songan   Munduk
NORTH AND   Bawan
WEST BALI   GUNUNG   2   Bukit
  p144   BATUR   Toya   Paleg
                          1,720 m   Bungkah
          3 21 KINTAMANI (5,643 ft)
                                        Trunyan
    PURA ULUN   Lake   Gunung
    DANU BATUR   Batur   Abang
Binyan   Penelokan   Abang
                                  Kedisan
Bunutin   BAYUNG GEDE 7   KARANGASEM
          VILLAGE 22 BANGLI   Suter
Meka   Bonyoh Pengotan
Tengah   BANGLI
                   Pelaktiying   Bukit
Sengkaduan   Tanahnui
                                                    GUNUNG
Pisang Kaja   Kayuambua   AGUNG
Bunteh   Bangkled   19
          Malet Seri Batu
    Bonjaka   Tiga   3,014 m
                  Kayubihi   Pempatan   (9,888 ft)
Manukaya   Kayang   Sebudi
                              Menanga   Sukaluih
Tampak Siring   Rendang   Muncan
                        Tegalsuci   Selat   Duda   Sibetan
Tegallalang   Bukit   Sekar   Putung
Kelabangmoding   Bangli   Unda 8
          Demulih Bebalang   ISEH   Telengan   Manggis
CENTRAL BALI   Gaga   Gembalan SIDEMEN   Sengkidu
  p90   9   Tanahampo
                  Bunutin   Talibeng Kaler   Amuk
Ubud   Jagaperang   Bay
GIANYAR   Sidan Tihingan   Besar
Peliatan Bedulu   Peteluan   4 KLUNGKUNG   14 PADANG BAI
                  KLUNG-   GOA LAWAH 11
Blahbatuh Gianyar KUNG GELGEL 10 BAT CAVE TEMPLE
          Serongga   Kusamba
Batuan   Klotak   Badung
                                     Strait

BESAKIH TEMPLE
COMPLEX 1

EAST BALI

Must Sees
1. Besakih Temple Complex
2. Gunung Batur
3. Pura Ulun Danu Batur
4. Klungkung
5. Tenganan Bali Aga Village

Experience More
6. Tirtagangga Palace
7. Bangli
8. Iseh
9. Sidemen
10. Gelgel
11. Goa Lawah Bat Cave Temple
12. Candidasa
13. Ujung
14. Padang Bai
15. Tulamben
16. Amlapura
17. Pura Lempuyang
18. Amed
19. Gunung Agung
20. Pura Tegeh Koripan
21. Kintamani
22. Bayung Gede Village

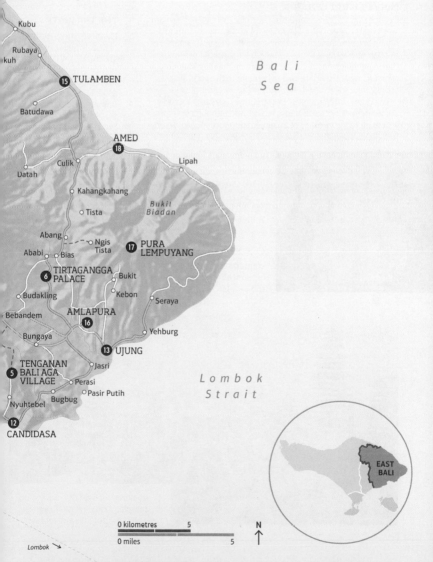

B a l i
S e a

turinggit

Kubu

Rubaya
kuh

15 TULAMBEN

Batudawa

AMED
18

Culik   Lipah

Datah

Kahangkahang

Tista   *Bukit*
             Biadan

Abang   Ngis
         Tista
Ababi   Bias   17 PURA
                     LEMPUYANG
TIRTAGANGGA
6 PALACE   Bukit

Budakling   Kebon
                        Seraya
Bebandem
         AMLAPURA
Bungaya 16
                   Yehburg
            13 UJUNG
TENGANAN   Jasri
5 BALI AGA
  VILLAGE   Perasi   *L o m b o k*
                         S t r a i t
Nyuhtebel Bugbug
         Pasir Putih
12
CANDIDASA

0 kilometres   5
0 miles   5

N
↑

Lombok

EAST
BALI

❶ ✍ Ⓜ ▭ 🏛

BESAKIH TEMPLE COMPLEX

🅐 F2 🏠 Besakih, Rendang, Karangasem Regency 🚌 ℹ️ Jalan Diponoegoro, Amlapura; (0363) 21 196 🕐 Dawn to dusk daily

For more than 1,000 years, Pura Besakih, Bali's most sacred, impressive, powerful and austere place of worship, has rested at an altitude of 900 metres (3,000 ft) on Mount Agung's southwestern slope. Known as the "Mother Temple", this sprawling complex comprises 22 temples united through ritual and history into a single sanctuary.

Holy Place of Worship

Overlooking stunning scenery of rice fields, hills, valleys, streams and forests beneath the watchful gaze of the mighty Gunung Agung volcano, Besakih's setting gives it a mystical quality. For the Balinese, visiting the complex is a truly special pilgrimage. Every day, hundreds of devout Hindus can be seen solemnly climbing a giant stairway to pay homage to the gods in an atmosphere thick with the smoke and scent of burning incense.

The many different temples and shrines vary considerably according to their status and function, and although you can visit most of them, many of the inner courtyards are reserved for religious pilgrims and are closed to the public. Most of the temples cluster around Pura Penataran Agung, the largest and most important sanctuary in the complex. The highest temple, Pura Pengubengan, lies amidst beautiful groves within a pine forest.

←

Woman standing at the top of the stairs in a gateway in the Besakih Temple Complex

THE TRIMURTI

Meaning "three forms of God" in Sanskrit, the Trimurti is the Hindu trinity. These three principal deities are especially revered in Bali. Pura Besakih is said to be their home. Pura Penataran Agung, with white banners, is dedicated to Shiva, the destroyer, in charge of ignorance; Pura Batu Madeg, with black banners, represents Vishnu, the preserver, in charge of balancing good and evil; and Pura Kiduling Kreteg has red banners and is devoted to Brahma, the creator, in charge of passion.

↑ Looking out over the roofs of the temples of Pura Besakih against a backdrop of hills and forests

Did You Know?

Besakih is Bali's only temple open to all devotees of any caste group.

↑ Worshipper climbing the stairway to the Pura Besakih Temple Complex

Pura Penataran Agung

The Great Temple of State, Pura Penataran Agung is the central, the largest and the most dramatic building in the complex due to its size, position and the great reverence in which it is held. Originating probably as a single, prehistoric shrine, it is the symbolic centre of Besakih, arranged on six levels terraced up the slope, which represent the six layers of the universe, each with their own shrines.

As worshippers climb the giant stairway lined with figures from the Hindu epics – the *Mahabarata* and the *Ramayana* – and pass through the first courtyard, they symbolically sever their connection with the everyday world. In all, there are 57 structures within this temple, about half of which are devoted to various deities, while others have various ceremonial functions, such as providing seating for the priests and the gamelan orchestra. Visitors may not be allowed inside all of the courtyards.

💬 INSIDER TIP
Beware of Scams

Unfortunately, Besakih is crippled by a cartel of unregulated guides and bullying touts offering tours at over-inflated prices. Bring your own sarong and sash, so that you don't have to rent one. To avoid the touts, enter via the left-hand side entrance rather than the central one.

↑ Visitors on the steps leading to Pura Penataran Agung

The tall meru *are shrines for deified kings, ancestral spirits and nature gods.*

The main courtyard is the principal focus of worship. A padmasana tiga (triple lotus shrine) is *dedicated to Brahma, Shiva and Vishnu.*

The terraces at the entrance to Pura Penataran Agung are an echo of the stepped pyramids of Indonesian prehistory.

→
Pura Penataran Agung, the spiritual core of the Besakih complex

The grand main entrance stairway leading to the temple

Footpaths connect the temples in the complex.

↑ Ceremonial gongs played during religious rituals

The inner courtyards of the temple may have contained meru towers since the 14th century.

Low walls surround the temple; visitors can view the shrines by walking along the footpaths and looking over the walls.

↑ Courtyard inside the temple; roof of a shrine *(inset)* in front of a *candi bentar* (split gate)

2 🌮 🍴 🖥 🛍

GUNUNG BATUR

🅰 F2 🚌 From Penelokan & Kintamani 🚤 From Kedisan 🛈 Jalan Letulila 9, Bangli, (0366) 91 537; Toya Bungkah Mount Batur Trekking Guides Office, (0366) 52 362

Rising to 1,717 m (5,633 ft), Gunung Batur draws visitors to its summit for the stunning panorama of Bali. Part of its spectacular caldera is filled with Lake Batur, Bali's largest crater lake. Superb views of the volcano can be enjoyed from the nearby village of Penelokan.

Although Gunung Batur is not the largest volcano in Bali, it is the most active. It is surrounded by a massive caldera, which implies that it was once much larger than now, having blown off its top in an eruption. It has erupted on a large scale more than 20 times in the last 200 years. The most devastating occasion was in 1917 when more than 1,000 people died and over 2,000 temples were destroyed. Volcanic activity has made the slopes of Gunung Batur bare and dry, in contrast to the vegetation which covers the slopes of Gunung Abang, on the opposite side of Lake Batur.

The fascinating Batur Geopark Museum (open 8am–5pm daily) at Penelokan near the volcano's crater rim, explains the geology of the volcano through detailed interactive displays and rock samples.

Climbing Gunung Batur

Most visitors use trails that start near Toya Bungkah village. Trekking to the top of Gunung Batur from here typically takes two hours. You can hire a local guide at the Mount Batur Trekking Guides office in the village. The most popular treks are timed for arrival at the summit at dawn to see the sunrise. The air can be quite chilly before daybreak, and warm clothing is highly recommended for night treks. You'll also need a torch. Guides will provide breakfast on the summit for a fee, which can include cooking an egg in the steaming holes at the top of the volcano. The slopes of the volcano can be slippery and dangerous in the rainy season from October to April, and trekking is not recommended during this time.

TRUNYAN BALI AGA VILLAGE

One of the culturally isolated Bali Aga villages, Trunyan is perched on the eastern shore of Lake Batur and is most easily accessible by boat from Kedisan. Villagers here practise customs found nowhere else in Bali. These include neolithic funeral rites. Instead of burying or cremating dead bodies, the people place them in pits covered by bamboo canopies to preserve them from being eaten by animals. The forces of nature dissolve the body tissues until only the skeleton remains. Trunyan is also known for the impressive Pura Pancering Jagat temple, inside which is a tall statue of the patron guardian of the village.

↑ Sunrise behind Mount Batur, a truly spectacular sight

1 Swimmers enjoying a geothermally heated hot spring at Toya Bungkah village at the foot of Mount Batur.

2 Lake Batur is the main source of irrigation for much of the agriculture of Central and East Bali.

3 Hikers descend friable terrain in the caldera of Mount Batur volcano.

3

PURA ULUN DANU BATUR

E2 Jalan Kintamani, Batur Selatan, Kintamani
Daily during daylight hours

This is the second-most-important temple complex in Bali after Besakih *(p116)*. Sitting on the southwestern rim of the Mount Batur caldera, it features nine graceful temples and many shrines.

INSIDER TIP
Dewi Danu

On the northeastern shore of Lake Batur is a striking yellow statue of Dewi Danu standing on a lotus flower and sea serpent. It can only be accessed by boat - for a small fee, a local boatman from Songan will take visitors across.

Lake Goddess

Ulun Danu literally translates as "head of the lake" and the temple is dedicated to Dewi Danu, the life-sustaining and highly venerated goddess of the lake, who supplies water to the 37 rivers, tributaries, dams and irrigation canals between here and the sea. Lake Batur is the source of dozens of underground springs, which help regulate the flow of water for the farmlands and sacred bathing pools throughout Gianyar and Bangli. Farmers from all over the island come here to pay homage to the goddess who helps bless the island's soil with fertility.

Main gateway to Pura Penataran Agung Batur, the principal temple in the complex ↑

OFFERINGS TO THE LAKE GODDESS

Devotees from all over Bali present elaborate offerings at Pura Ulun Danu Batur. The respect accorded to the goddess of Lake Batur is reinforced by events in the temple's history. At its former location closer to the lake at the foot of the Batur volcano, the temple was miraculously saved from destruction in the volcanic eruption of 1917, when the lava flow stopped just short of its walls. Another eruption, in 1926, prompted the villagers to move it to its present location at the highest and oldest rim of the caldera.

The nine-temple complex, with its impressive tall gateway, contains a maze of more than 200 shrines and pavilions dedicated to the gods and goddesses of water, agriculture, holy springs, arts and crafts. In the northwest corner, a Chinese-style shrine flanked by colourful statues is dedicated to Ida Ratu Ayu Subandar, god of merchants.

$\longrightarrow$

Tops of gates in Pura Ulun Danu Batur, with Mount Batur in the background

Pura Penataran Agung Batur

With five main courtyards, Pura Penataran Agung Batur is the principal temple in the Pura Ulun Danu Batur complex. The dominant shrines are the pagoda-like *merus*, the most significant of which is the 11-tiered *meru* in the inner courtyard, dedicated to Dewi Danu. There are also three nine-tiered *merus* for the gods of Mount Batur, Mount Agung and Ida Batara Dalem Baturenggong, the 15th-century deified king of Gelgel. The *kulkul* (drum) tower in the outer courtyard houses a wooden split drum that is beaten 45 times each morning to honour the 45 deities worshipped in the temple.

Did You Know?

The main festival here takes place on the 10th full moon in the Balinese calendar (late Mar-early Apr).

→
Layout of the Pura Penataran Agung Batur, with its impressive architectural structures

The third courtyard is the most sacred. Three gateways lead from one courtyard to the next.

The figure of Garuda, a bird from Hindu mythology, is depicted in this stone relief on the courtyard wall.

The great quadrangular central courtyard is the occasional setting for baris gede, *an old ritual dance performed by a regiment of soldiers to protect the deities.*

←
A few of the pavilions and *merus* in Pura Penataran Agung Batur

① Ornate, gold-painted carvings feature on the great timber doors of the main temple gateway.

② Offerings are carried to the Lake Goddess Dewi Danu by devotees.

③ This beautiful side gate is built in a combination of brickwork and carved stone decoration.

The great timber doors of the main temple gateway are reserved for the use of priests on important occasions.

This tall, slender side gate leads to another temple.

Entrance

The bale gong is a pavilion housing the temple's set of gamelan instruments, including a great gong believed to have a magical history.

↑ The Puputan monument, fashioned in dark stone, opposite Taman Gili

④ 🍴 🖥 🛍

KLUNGKUNG

⚑ F3 🚍 ℹ jalan Untung Surapati 3; 0366 21 448

The royal capital of Bali's smallest regency, Klungkung (also known as Semarapura), was the focal point of art and culture during the Gelgel dynasty. In the centre of this bustling trade town is the Taman Gili, the remains of the 18th-century royal palace.

① Puputan Monument

⚐ Corner of Jalan Untung Surapati and Jalan Gajah Maja

In 1908, Klungkung was the last kingdom in Bali holding out against the rule of the Dutch invaders. Hopelessly outnumbered, the raja of Klungung, accompanied by 200 members of his family and court, made a desperate sortie out of his palace into the face of the Dutch guns. The raja was armed with a *kris* (dagger) that, according to a prophesy, was supposed to wreak havoc upon the enemy. However, the *kris* failed to fulfill the desired outcome, and the raja was shot by a Dutch bullet. His six wives promptly committed ritual suicide, or *puputan*, each killing herself with her own *kris*, followed by all the other members of the court. The sacrifice is commemorated in the tall Puputan Monument.

② Museum Daerah Semarapura

⚐ Corner of Jalan Surapati and Jalan Puputan
☎ (0878) 6246 6055
🕐 8am–5pm daily

To the west of Taman Gili, the small Museum Daerah Semarapura contains old Dutch newspapers recounting the sickening details of the *puputan* massacre in 1908, when 200 members of Klungkung's royal court committed ritual suicide. Interesting exhibits also include the royal litter carriage *(palanquin)*, which was bearing the raja when the Dutch opened fire, as well as photos of the raja with his family and the royal court.

③ Pura Taman Sari

⚐ Jl Ahmad Jani
🕐 Dawn to dusk daily

The 17th-century Pura Taman Sari temple is a serene place to relax. The name means flower garden and the temple features grassy compounds planted with flowers, and a grey-stone eleven-roofed *meru* surrounded by a waterlily-filled moat.

④ Klungkung Market

⚐ Jalan Puputan 7 🕐 6am–6pm daily

Hidden in a concrete building to the east of Kerta Gosa, is Klungkung's fabric market, an Aladdin's cave for lovers of traditional textiles. Vendors sell *songket* (a rich brocade) in a wide variety of designs, as well as another of Bali's authentic fabrics, *endek*, for a much lower price than you'd pay elsewhere.

⑤
Kamasan

🚗 **1.6 km (1 mile) south of Klungkung**

The village of Kamasan is a community of artists. Their work is in the *wayang* style that is found on the Kerta Gosa ceilings of the former royal palace (*p128*), and only Kamasan artists are allowed to restore the frescoes today.

The rigidly standardised, formal style is strictly flat, one-dimensional and beautifully decorative with rich colours and intricate patterns. Faces are drawn in three-quarters profile, similar to shadow puppets against a screen, and there is no central focal

point, yet each painting tells multiple stories. Kamasan art originally had religious themes, and the artists were sent all over Bali to decorate temples and palaces. It was Bali's only form of pictorial representation until the 20th century, when European artists arrived and influenced the Balinese to paint realistic scenes of everyday life.

During Dutch rule, the Kamasan artists lost their royal patronage and their

specific style of art nearly died. Happily, Kamasan underwent a resurgence when the Dutch commissioned the restoration of the Kerta Gosa paintings in the 1920s and '30s. Since the 1960s, tourists and art shops have been an important source of revenue. You can still buy these cloth paintings, unframed and at very reasonable prices, in various shops in the village. Be generous; these fine traditional artists are an endangered species.

BALINESE ENDEK

The most common traditional textile in Bali is *endek*, a form of weft *ikat*. A motif is dyed into the threads of a cloth before it is woven using a resist-dye method. Repeated tying and dyeing produces a textile of shimmering multi-hued patterns. In Bali the designs are applied only to the weft threads.

⑥
Tihingan

🚗 **4 km (2.5 miles) west of Klungkung**

The centre of production of Balinese gamelan musical instruments, Tihingan village welcomes visitors at craftsmen's workshops. Here you can observe the techniques of the blacksmiths, known as *besalen* and *pande gong,* as they forge, bend and weld metal pieces into gongs and metallophones, and fine-tune each to the perfect pitch. Ritual brass and copper instruments are also crafted, such as the bells used by Balinese priests. As well as making metal gamelan instruments, the master craftsmen also create beautiful pedestals and traditional two-sided drums.

⑦ 🗺 🏞

TAMAN GILI

🏠 Puri Semarapura, corner of Jalan Surapati and Jalan Puputan, Klungkung 🕐 7am–6pm daily 🚫 Public holidays

Dating to the early 18th century, Taman Gili ("moated garden") is what remains of Klungkung's royal palace. The paintings in the Bale Kerta Gosa and Bale Kambang are beautiful examples of the *wayang* style.

Most of of the royal palace was destroyed in 1908 during the Dutch conquest. The main surviving features are two raised, open meeting halls, or *bale*, with intricately painted ceilings. The painted panels arranged in several tiers have undergone restoration and repainting several times in the last hundred years. They follow the traditional *wayang* style, in which the figures resemble shadow puppets (*p127*). The present structure of the Bale Kambang dates from the 1940s.

This palace was built along traditional lines – Balinese palaces are not huge standalone buildings, but rather a series of courtyards, gilded pavilions, gardens, rice sheds and family temples, linked by a tranquil maze of gateways and alleyways, and enclosed by high walls. Because Balinese kingdoms were defined, not by borders, but by their social and economic hub – the palace was centrally located near the market, which was the focus of artistic and economic activity.

At the apex of the ceiling is a carved lotus flower surrounded by gilded doves, representing the goals of enlightenment and salvation.

There are 267 painted panels arranged in several tiers in the Kerta Gosa.

Entrance

← The peaceful Taman Gili palace, with its pavilions, courtyards, stone statues and bridges

KERTA GOSA CEILING PAINTINGS

The main series shows part of the *Bhima Swarga* narrative, which was incorporated into Balinese tradition from the Indian *Mahabharata* epic. There are also scenes from the *Tantri* stories (a Balinese version of Indian moral fables), and some are based on an astrological calendar, showing earthquakes and eruptions.

Layout of the buildings and gardens forming the Taman Gili royal palace complex

Did You Know?

The main gate is said to have shut on its own after the 1908 *puputan*. Nobody has dared to open it since.

The roof of the Bale Kambang is made of hardwood shingles.

The ceiling paintings in the Bale Kambang depict scenes from Balinese myths, including the story of Sutasoma, a Buddhist saint symbolizing strength without aggression.

The moat surrounding Bale Kambang teems with carp.

The building is surrounded by many carved stone reliefs of mythical creatures.

→ A stone statue of an ancient mythical demon in Taman Gili

⑤ ◈ ◈ ▭ ⏁

TENGANAN BALI AGA VILLAGE

🅐 G3 🅐 3 km (2 miles) west of Candidasa 🚍 From Candidasa 🅘 Amlapura; (0363) 21 196 🕓 Dawn–dusk

Step back in time at Tenganan village, home to the ancient Bali Aga people. Descendants of the original Balinese, the Bali Aga inhabited Bali before the arrival of the Majapahit in the 11th century.

The Bali Aga resisted the rule of the Majapahit kings, fiercely safeguarding and maintaining their own culture through the conviction that they are descended from the gods.

A visit here is one of Bali's most authentic cultural experiences. One of the island's original pre-Hindu settlements, the village is still a stronghold of native traditions and the Bali Aga maintain a lifestyle bound by strict *adat* (customary law) practices. A tiny socialist republic, all of the village and surrounding fertile farmland is owned communally. The rice fields are rented out to other farms and profits are evenly divided among the villagers.

The villagers are thus able to devote their time to crafts, including cloth-weaving, calligraphy and basket-weaving. In particular, *geringsing* – double *ikat* textiles – are woven here. The ritually significant cloth is believed to protect the wearer from sickness and evil vibrations. Cars and motorcycles are foribidden from entering the village.

① Traditional calligraphy is inscribed onto palm leaf manuscripts.

② Offerings are presented at traditional ceremonies.

③ Double *ikat* weaving is used to create *geringsing* cloth.

THE LEGEND OF TENGANAN

It is said that in the 14th century, King Bedaulu, the ruler of Bali, lost his favourite horse and offered a reward for its return. The horse was eventually found dead near Tenganan and the villagers asked to be granted land as a reward. In spite of the fact that the horse was dead, the King sent his minister to draw the boundaries of the area to be given to them, instructing the minister to include all of the land where he could smell the dead horse. Accompanied by the village chief, who had cunningly hidden some of the rotting horse meat in his clothes, the minister performed his duties and drew generous boundaries which remain today.

← Street in Tenganan, where the Bali Aga strictly adhere to a traditional way of life of ritual and ceremony

Exploring Tenganan Bali Aga Village

The most striking feature of this neat, walled village is its unique layout. Open-sided community halls and elevated longhouses, including the stately Bale Agung, where the council of elders makes its decisions, have been meticulously positioned in accordance with long-established beliefs. Three parallel avenues run north to south, ascending towards the mountains, each level connected by steep cobbled ramps, while narrow lanes run east to west forming a grid. Single-storey dwellings line both sides of the main street, along with rice barns, shrines, communal pavilions, open kitchens and *bale* administration buildings.

In front of many houses, traditional *ata* vine baskets are laid out in neat rows to dry in the sun. Demonstrations of weaving and other crafts can be seen inside the villagers' houses, which also function as shops and workshops. You can watch calligraphers inscribe elaborate calendars and illustrations on palm leaves with ink brewed from burnt macadamia nuts, weavers create intricate *geringsing* textiles and woodcarvers make masks.

At the northern end of the village, beyond the elementary school, an arched gate opens onto a jungle of towering breadfruit and durian trees, coconut palms and hanging creepers. A few steps up the hill is the beekeeper's house, where visitors are always welcome.

In the village's "temple of origins", the community joins in rituals reflecting a dualistic cosmology based on principles of complementary opposites.

The *wantilan* is a large, open pavilion where village members meet for social activities.

The main streets are partly cobbled and rise in tiers, connected by ramps.

← Bali Aga women carrying harvested coconuts; rice fields surrounding the village, which are worked by neighbouring farmers *(inset)*

MEKARE-KARE

The *mekare-kare* is an annual theatrical fight in June between the young men of the village using prickly pandanus leaf whips. Each dual is staged to the martial sounds of gamelan *selonding* music and lasts only a few seconds, accompanied by much merriment and laughter. The attacks are warded off with tightly woven *ata* vine shields; there are no winners and no losers because the objective is to draw blood as an offering to the gods. After the battles, the combatants' wounds are treated with alcohol and turmeric, leaving no scars.

Market

The Bale Petemu is the meeting hall of one of three associations of unmarried village men.

The village houses have steps and a courtyard.

Did You Know?

Tenganan crafts are also sold in specialist shops in Seminyak and Ubud.

←

Plan of the well-preserved Tenganan Bali Aga Village

The kitchen of the Bale Agung is where ceremonial meals are cooked.

Entrance

The Bale Agung is the hall for meetings of the village council, composed of all the married couples.

Beautiful terraced rice fields around Tirtagangga, with Gunung Lempuyang and Gunung Seraya in the background ↑

A LONG WALK
TENGANAN TO TIRTAGANGGA

Distance 6 km (4 miles) **Walking time** 3 hours
Nearest town Candidasa **Transport** Bemo to
Candidasa, then own transport **Terrain** Hilly

The walk from Tenganan to Tirtagangga reveals
some of the most scenic terrain of Bali's interior, and
many glimpses of traditional Balinese life along the
way. From the higher points there are impressive
views of Bali's mountains; the route also passes
through terraced rice fields and peaceful hillside
villages with beautiful temples.

Ababi

Bukit
Tiragangga
302 m
(990 ft)

Tirtagangga
FINISH

*The country road
to **Tirtagangga**
offers good views
of rice fields with
the sea beyond.*

Bukit Komala
△ 393 m
(1,289 ft)

Krotok

△
Bukit Dausa
283 m
(928 ft)

Budakeling

0 kilometres 1

0 miles 1

N

Bebandem

*The metal-smithing village
of **Budakeling** is north of
the main road before you
arrive at a lava trail.*

*A small café, or hillside
warung, stands on the
slope overlooking the rice
terraces. The trail leads on
to an irrigation dam and a
rice field shrine before
crossing a shallow river.*

△
Bukit
Sangyangapi
287 m
(941 ft)

Kastala

Hillside Warung

*Across the river, the trail
leads to **Kastala village**
near the main road. To cut
short the walk, transport can
be taken from Bebandem.*

Bungaya
Kangin

Gumung
Kaja

Pura Puseh

*In the village of
Gumung Kaja, baskets
and mats are woven
with the stems of the
ata, a kind of palm tree.*

*At the **Pura Puseh** temple, a
view to the far east of Bali is
revealed; rice fields can be
seen at various
stages of cultivation.*

Bungaya Kauh

△
Bukit
Kauh
263 m
(862 ft)

*From the **Tenganan
village** gate, a stone-paved
path leads to a temple
complex and then to the
edge of the forest.*

EAST BALI

Tenganan to
Tirtagangga
•

Tenganan

START

Tenganan
Village Gate

Dauh
Tukad

△
Bukit Kangin
315 m
(1,033 ft)

Locator Map
For more detail see p114

135

EXPERIENCE MORE

6 (slash) (M) (Y) (A)

Tirtagangga Palace

A G3 **H** Ababi **C** (0361) 730 374 **=** **O** Daily

Tirtagangga (meaning "holy water from the Ganges") is the best surviving example of Bali's royal water palaces. It was built in 1947 by Anak Agung Anglurah Ketut, the last king of Karangasem. The complex consists of a sacred spring, a cold spring-fed pool and several other ponds, all set in lovely gardens. Bathing is permitted in the pools. A small fee is charged at the spring-fed pool, which has simple changing rooms.

Tirtagangga has a cool climate, and is a good base for walks in the area. There are several homestays here.

___

7 (Y) (D) (A)

Bangli

A F3 **=** **i** Jalan Brigjen Ngurah Rai 30; (0366) 91 537

A royal court city from the 14th to the 19th century, Bangli is one of Bali's oldest towns, a small, well-ordered and tidy community set some

way up the hills towards Gunung Batur – ideal for a walk in the cool mountain air.

Pura Kehen, a place of worship since the 12th century, steps impressively up a hillside in a series of eight terraces. A huge banyan tree in the first courtyard of the complex conceals an almost invisible *kulkul* – an alarm drum – high in its branches. Fine statuary lines the steps leading to the *padmasana* shrine where there is a multitiered *meru* roof in the inner sanctuary. The shrine is elaborately ornamented and the gold painted doors of the temple are beautiful. Entry is with a donation.

Pura Penyimpenan ("the temple for keeping things") contains three ancient bronze inscriptions which imply that the area was considered holy long before the present temple complex was built.

Images of heaven and hell, the latter imaginatively grim, cover the walls of **Pura Dalem Pengungekan**, a temple

---

TEXTILES OF EAST BALI

In Bali great importance is attached to textiles and their making. This area is famous for a type of double ikat weave called *geringsing*, produced only in the Bali Aga village of Tenganan *(p130)* and credited by the Balinese with protective spiritual powers. In Sidemen complex, decorative motifs in gold and silver threads are woven into cloth to create a rich brocade textile known as *songket*. This is often worn at religious or social events, and as part of the costume of traditional dancers.

← Stepping stones and statuary across the royal ponds at Tirtagangga Palace

great volcanic valleys. The terraced rice fields are lush and green. Iseh itself is a small village with little in the way of tourist facilities. Walter Spies (p56) built a house here (now a luxurious rental property), and it was this location that inspired some of his most beautiful paintings.

At Putung, 6 km (4 miles) east of Iseh, there are some great lookout points and a couple of homestays. A further 4 km (2 miles) to the east is the village of Sibetan, the best place to buy *salak*, a small, crisp, tart-tasting fruit with a scaly exterior that looks rather like snakeskin.

9 🍴 🏞

Sidemen

🗺 **F3** 🚌 **From Bangli and Klungkung** ℹ **Amlapura; (0363) 21 196**

Sidemen is set in some of the most beautiful countryside in East Bali. The views from the slopes of Gunung Agung stretch out like a green patchwork with an impressive mountain backdrop. The town is a retreat from the hustle and bustle elsewhere, and

---

📷 PICTURE PERFECT
House Beautiful

The house built by artist Walter Spies at Iseh, now a hotel, is blessed with a breathtaking view of the Sidemen Valley and Gunung Agung, one that has been enjoyed by many famous guests, including Mick Jagger and David Bowie.

---

there are some good home-stays overlooking rice fields. In Sidemen you can visit workshops making *songket*. This work is historically the preserve of higher castes, and still implies high social status.

10

Gelgel

🗺 **F3** 🚌 **From Klungkung** ℹ **Klungkung; (0366) 21 448**

The royal court of the Majapahit rulers of Bali (p54) was established in Gelgel in the 14th century by Dewa Ketut Ngulesir, son of Bali's first Majapahit king. A reminder of the former king-dom is Gelgel's ancient royal temple of Pura Dasar, with its large outer courtyard, and several tall *meru* towers.

The Pura Penataran is one of several temples along the village's broad streets.

---

dedicated to the dead, and inside are shrines to Brahma, Shiva and Vishnu.

Pura Kehen
🗺 Jalan Sri Wijaya ⏰ Daily

Pura Penyimpenan
🗺 Jalan Sri Wijaya ⏰ Daily
🚫 For ceremonies

Pura Dalem Pengungekan
🗺 Jalan Merdeka ⏰ Daily
🚫 For ceremonies

---

8 🏞
Iseh

🗺 **F3** 🚌 **From Bangli and Klungkung** ℹ **Amlapura; (0363) 21 196**

The area around Iseh is remarkable for glorious landscapes. Some of the best can be seen on the road eastward from Bangli via Muncan and Duda, which carves its way east through

→ The magnificent Gunung Agung, viewed from across the Sidemen Valley

⑪ 🍴 🍽 🛍

Goa Lawah Bat Cave Temple

🅰F3 📧 ℹKlungkung; (0363) 21 448 ⊙Daily

Thought to be more than 1,000 years old, Goa Lawah is important to temple rituals pertaining to the afterlife. The main feature of the temple is a cave inhabited by tens of thousands of fruit bats. Local legend has it that the cave stretches 30 km (19 miles) back into the mountain, as far as Besakih (p116), and is the home of a giant dragon-like snake called Basuki who feasts on bats.

There are some good eateries outside the cave that have fine views over the ocean towards Nusa Penida and Lombok. However, it is also renowned for hawkers.

Kusamba, 4 km (3 miles) southwest of Goa Lawah, is a busy little fishing village with a black-sand beach. *Jukung* (outrigger fishing craft) line the shore, and are available for chartered day trips to nearby islands. Be aware that the sea can be quite choppy. Salt production pans can be seen here.

─────────────

⑫

Candidasa

🅰G3 📧 ℹJalan Candidasa; (0363) 21 002

The fishing village of Candidasa is an ideal base for diving, snorkelling, trekking and exploring Bali's peaceful east coast. This beautiful area in the royal Balinese regency of Karangasem boasts a rich heritage. Here, life goes on as it has for generations. It is a quieter place than other built-up tourist areas in Bali, but still has a full range of accomodation options, as well as spas and restaurants.

The name Candidasa was originally applied just to two small temples, one dedicated to Siwa, and the other, on a sacred palm-fringed lagoon beside the beach, to Hariti, goddess of fertility. This is a place of worship for childless couples; the name Candidasa is said to be derived from the Balinese "Cilidasa", which means "ten children".

In the Blue Lagoon bay, the water is clear and warm, with abundant marine life amid a coral reef, making it ideal for snorkelling and diving. The hiking around Candidasa is also superb. From Bukit Asah near the village of Bugbug, a

↑ Underwater encounter with a shoal of soldierfish at the reef off Candidasa

30-minute walk brings you to a hilltop outlook with a beautiful panorama of the sea, the coastline and neighbouring islands. From here, it is just another 10 minutes to Pasir Putih (known as Virgin Beach), a gorgeous, 500-m (550-yard) stretch of sand fringed with coconut palms. Grass-roofed *warungs* offer cold drinks and fresh fish. Visitors can rent sunbeds and umbrellas, and enjoy beach massages.

13

Ujung

G3 From Amlapura
Amlapura; (0363) 21196

Ujung, meaning "at the end", is an appropriate name given the remote location of this fishing village. The Puri Taman Ujung is a water palace built in 1919 by the last raja of Karangasem, Anak Agung Anglurah Ketut. The buildings were all but destroyed in the 1976 earthquake but have been restored to their former grandeur.

The narrow road winding east from Ujung around the eastern tip of Bali is very scenic, with spectacular views of the ocean and Gunung Seraya. Before taking this road, it is advisable to check its condition with the locals.

---

14 🍴 🖥 🏠

Padang Bai

F3 To Nusa Lembongan, Nusa Penida & Lembar, Lombok
Amlapura; (0363) 21196

This beach resort makes a good base for exploration and is also the main port for

ferries to Lombok, so the traffic from Denpasar is quite heavy. In the village there are numerous restaurants, hotels, guesthouses, bars, tour guides and dive shops.

Within walking distance, to the west of Padang Bai, is Biastugal, an unspoiled white-sand bay where sun-worshippers gather. A little further along the coast it is possible to rent outriggers for diving and snorkelling. At the eastern end of the bay, a 20-minute walk away, there are several temples. They include Pura Silayukti, associated with Mpu Kuturan, who introduced the three-temple system to Balinese villages in the 11th century.

> In the Blue Lagoon bay, the water is clear and warm, with abundant marine life amid a coral reef, making it ideal for snorkelling and diving.

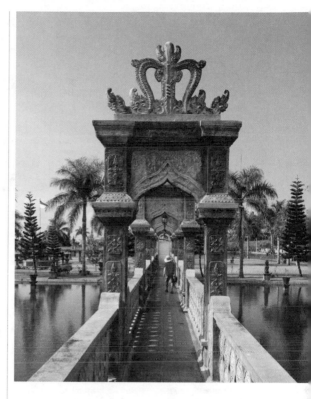

↑ Bridge leading to the main temple building at Puri Taman Ujung

15 🍴 🖥 🏠

Tulamben

G2 From Amlapura & Singaraja Amlapura; (0363) 21196

Tulamben is a nondescript little village, but it is of interest as the location of the wreck of the American cargo ship *Liberty*, 120 m (396 ft) long and torpedoed during World War II. It lies 40 m (44 yards) offshore and, at its deepest point, some 60 m (198 ft) down. The wreck is now covered in coral and inhabited by fish. The water provides great diving and snorkelling. Day trips off Tulamben can be arranged with dive operators. Boats can be rented locally.

European decorative ↑
influence at the royal
palace at Amlapura

Amlapura

G3 | **Jalan
Diponegoro; (0363) 21 196**

The small but busy trading
town of Amlapura is a district
capital with an active market
serving the area. The town
was given its present name
after reconstruction in the
aftermath of the 1963
eruption of Gunung Agung. It
is still often referred to by its
former name, Karangasem.

Karangasem became an
important power in the late
17th century. The royal
families of Karangasem had
strong political links with the
nearby island of Lombok.
Puri Agung, a royal palace
of the kings of Karangasem,
was built at the turn of the
20th century. It was the
birthplace of the last king.

Did You Know?

Made from Balinese
cocoa beans and
minimally processed,
Sorga Chocolate
is truly delicious.

The palace compound is no
longer inhabited, descendants
of the royal family preferring
to live in the palaces of Puri
Gede and Puri Kertasurahe
across the road (unlike Puri
Agung, these are not open to
the public). Architecturally,
Puri Agung is an eclectic mix
of European and Balinese
styles. It has a particularly
impressive entrance gateway.

The main attraction is
the Maskerdam Building
("Amsterdam" as pronounced
by the locals), so-called as a
tribute to the Dutch following
their conquest of Lombok in
1894, when Karangasem
placed itself under Dutch rule.
Behind its carved doors are
pieces of furniture donated
by Queen Wilhelmina of the
Dutch royal family. Another
building is known as the Bale
London, as some of its
furniture bears the British
royal family's coat of arms.

Just south of Amlapuri,
in the beach resort of Jasri,
is a hidden gem: the small
artisanal **Sorga Chocolate
Factory**. Visitors can observe
the entire chocolate-making
process, from the harvesting
of the cacao fruits to the
finished, and delicious,
organic chocolate bars and
truffles (*sorga* means

"heaven"). A tasting session is
a must; chocolate-making
workshops are also on offer.

Puri Agung

| Jalan Sultan Agung
| Daily

Sorga Chocolate Factory

| Jalan Pura Mastima,
Jasri | 8am-5pm Mon-Sat,
8am-noon & 2-5pm Sun
| sorgachocolate.com

Pura Lempuyang

G2 | **Drive through the
villages of Tista, Abang and
Ngis Tista** | **Amlapura;
(0363) 21 196** | **Daily**

A visit to Pura Lempuyang
is well worth a full day trip,
especially when there is a
temple ceremony taking
place. Getting there is part of
the attraction – the road from
Tirtagangga runs northeast
along a picturesque valley,
carving its way through lush
rice fields. Pura Lempuyang is

→

The view through the
split gate at Pura Agung
Lempuyang Tara Penah

a complex of seven temples, the most spectacular of which is Pura Agung Lempuyang Tara Penah. Here, a dazzling-white, towering split gate perfectly frames Gunung Agung. The temple guardians – three pairs of colossal sea serpents – border a trio of towering staircases with Balinese doors at the top.

About 1 km (0.5 miles) further on, another temple, Pura Pasar Agung Lempuyang, marks a stairway of 1,700 steps, with strategic resting places along the way. It winds through the monkey-inhabited forest up to the directional temple of Lempuyang Luhur, 768 m (2,500 ft) above sea level to the southeast of Gunung Agung. It's not large – there is just a single courtyard – but it is one of Bali's oldest and most highly regarded temples, important because of its location. This has probably been a sacred site since pre-Hindu times, and the intense spiritual energy of this place is almost tangible. There's a story that in the 1960s, before electricity reached Bali, a space satellite reported the observation of a blue beam emanating from Earth; the precise location was plotted and the source was confirmed as Pura Lempuyang Luhur.

Amed

🅐 G2 🚌 ℹ️ Amlapura; (0363) 21196

Amed is the collective name given to a series of fishing villages that lie along about

10 km (6 miles) of the island's easternmost shore, via a rollercoaster of a road that coils around steep head-lands, sheltered coves and scalloped, grey-sand beaches cluttered with traditional *jukung* fishing boats. With fabulous sunset views of Gunung Agung and brilliant sunrises over Lombok, this laid-back area boasts some of the best coral reefs and dive sites on the island. It is also the start-point for trekking up the slopes of Gunung Seraya.

Dive resorts, hotels and restaurants are plentiful here. Salt production is carried out on the beach, and local fishermen take visitors out in their traditional boats.

The sleepy market village of Seraya itself is perched on the cliffs above the rocky coast. It is believed to be the first village to weave the sacred black-and-white chequered *poleng* cloth that you see all over Bali, draped around trees and statues and worn at ceremonies. The weaving industry has been revived here. The villagers grow natural dye plants such as morinda and indigo around the edges of their fields and you can watch the women weaving traditional Seraya textiles.

EAT

Warung Enak
This charming eatery serves fresh, authentic Balinese dishes.

🅐 G2 🏠 Purwakerti, Amed 📞 (0819) 1567 9019

Sails Restaurant
On a hillside with sea views, Sails offers Mediterranean cuisine.

🅐 G2 🏠 Bunutan, Amed 📞 (0363) 22 006

Aquaterrace
Delicious Indonesian and Pan-Asian dishes are served at this cliff-top restaurant.

🅐 G2 🏠 Selang Bunutan, Amed 🌐 aqua terrace-amed.com

19

Gunung Agung

Ⓐ F2

Mighty Gunung Agung, the highest point on Bali, is a 3,014-m (9,888-ft) active volcano, and the dominant feature of East Bali. The Balinese believe it to be an earthly replica of Mount Meru, central axis of the universe, and as such it has a profound significance in their lives. Communities orientate their houses, temples and even beds in relation to this sacred place, where the spirits of ancestors are thought to dwell.

The barren, lava-scoured eastern flanks of Gunung Agung bear witness to its most devastating eruption in recent history, in 1963. According to local belief, this was violent retribution for the mistiming of a lengthy religious ceremony that must be performed all over Bali every hundred years to placate the demon gods of danger.

However, the volcano is now active again and therefore, for reasons of safety, it is currently forbidden to climb Gunung Agung. But even on the lower slopes, visitors should be

---

THE POWER OF GUNUNG AGUNG

The Gunung Agung volcano belongs to the same class as Krakatoa, Vesuvius and Mount St Helens, and as such is capable of cataclysmic eruptions accompanied by the phenomenon of pyroclastic flow, in which a cloud of deadly burning gases powers down the mountainside ahead of the lava stream. The latest period of eruption activity, both seismic and volcanic, began in 2017, and prompted the evacuation of 122,500 people from their homes. An EDA (Estimated Danger Zone) of 6 km (4 miles) around the volcano has been in place since this time.

---

aware that they are in the vicinity of a holy place: observe the rules for temple dress (*p199*) and refrain from disrespectful behaviour.

20

Pura Tegeh Koripan

Ⓐ E1 🚌 From Kintamani
ℹ️ Penelokan; (0366) 51 370
🕐 Daily 🕐 During ceremonies

Also known as Pura Sukawana or Pura Penulisan, Pura Tegeh Koripan is one of the oldest temples in Bali, dating from the 11th century or earlier. Set at more than 1,500 m (4,950 ft) on the side of Gunung Penulisan, it is certainly one of the highest.

It is little visited by tourists and, therefore, has a peaceful atmosphere.

The site is in fact a complex of five temples. Its pyramidal structure, set on eleven levels of terraces along the slope, suggests that it dates from the pre-Hindu-Buddhist era, and is associated with the megalithic culture of Bali.

The main temple, Pura Panarajon, dedicated to the god of the mountains, is over 300 steps up, at the highest position in the complex. Inside, there are some stone inscriptions and statues thought to date to the 10th century.

From the slopes of Gunung Penulisan there are good views: on clear days you can see as far as Java to the east, and the Bali Sea to the north.

21 🍴 🍵 🛍️

Kintamani

🅰E2 🚌 ℹ️Penelokan; (0366) 51 370

One of the most popular destinations for visitors in Bali is Kintamani, notable above all for its view of a volcano within a caldera. The air here is fresh and the view from Kintamani into the caldera of Gunung Batur *(p120)* is perhaps the most famous on the island, as the tourist buses testify.

Kintamani is one of three small villages, along with Penelokan and Batur, set high on Batur's caldera rim. It is hard to distinguish where one ends and the next begins, as they have merged together to form a ribbon of development catering for the many visitors and tour buses that come here. Arriving early in the day helps avoid the crowds and provides the best photo opportunities as afternoons can be cloudy.

However, people do not come to look at the village of Kintamani itself – they come to stand in awe of the view. It is worth stopping here just to get a real sense of the scale of the landscape from a high vantage point; here it

is easy to see the relative positions of Gunung Batur, the Bali Aga village of Trunyan *(p121)* down on the shore of Lake Batur, and Gunung Abang on the eastern side of the lake facing Gunung Batur.

Lake Batur lies within a much more ancient caldera here, and is fed by hot springs; bathing facilities are offered at Toya Bungkah. There are many places to eat along most of the 10 km (6 miles) of the main road along the crater rim; there is also a volcano museum and a market selling fresh local produce.

↑ Floating pier with a bar and pleasure boats at Lake Batur, Kintamani

mud-brick walls, are home to more than 2,000 residents, and a protective wall of living bamboo surrounds the whole community. Roofs are made of interwoven bamboo tiles; when new roofs are needed, families and friends come together in *gotong royong* (shared work) to raise a new roof. Bayung Gede is the real deal, not a stage-managed tourist site. Nevertheless, visitors are welcomed here.

22

Bayung Gede Village

🅰E2 🏔️8 km (5 miles) southwest of Kintamani

The small village of Bayung Gede is a place where time has stood still. Believed to be the first village of the Bali Mula, the earliest inhabitants of the island, it dates back to pre-Hindu times and still maintains the traditions established by its founders. The village has a quiet pace and an almost complete lack of vehicular traffic. The north–south running streets, with their houses sheltered behind

←
Smoke and steam issuing from Gunung Agung during an active period

---

EAT

Bali Asli
This restaurant/ cooking school in the foothills of Gunung Agung offers glorious views. It serves traditional Balinese food created from home-grown produce and cooked in an authentic Balinese-style kitchen on wood-fired, mud-brick stoves.

🅰G2 🏠Jalan Raya Gelumpang, Gelumpang 🌐baliasli.com

Ⓡ Ⓡ Ⓡ

NORTH AND WEST BALI

This area corresponds to the regencies of Tabanan, Jembrana and Buleleng, of which the administrative capitals are Tabanan, Negara and Singaraja respectively. The population is increasingly Muslim as you move west; the older Muslim settlements were established by Bugis sailors in the 17th century who came to Bali to escape the Dutch invasion of Sulawesi in 1667.

The history of this part of Bali has been influenced as much by the sea as by the traditions of the courts: both Singaraja and Negara have the flavour more of Javanese coastal trading towns than of the Balinese centres of aristocratic power. North Bali is more heavily marked by the Dutch colonial presence than the rest of the island, which was colonized later. Following their brutal takeover of Buleleng in 1849, the Dutch set up a Residentie (prefecture) in Singaraja in 1855. Singaraja shows evidence of its Dutch past in its old offices and mansions and the airy, shady atmosphere of the town. New converts to Christianity were resettled by the Dutch in the hinterland of Negara. Later, several settlements were established along the coast by Madurese migrants.

NORTH AND WEST BALI

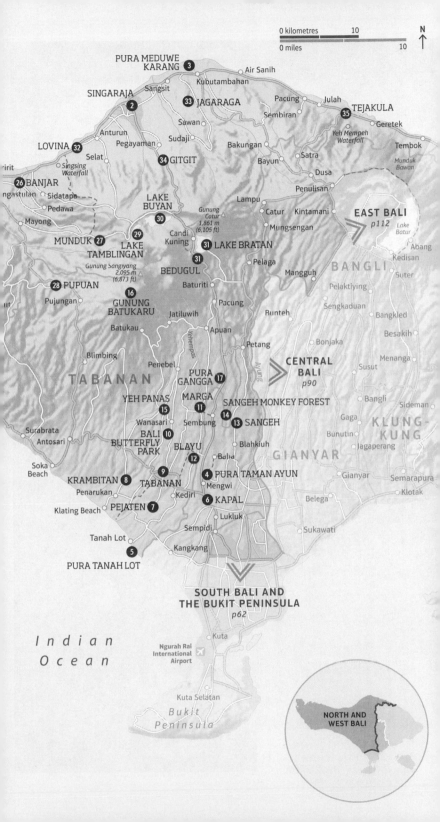

Platform above the dense tree canopy in The Menjangan Resort, Taman Nasional Bali Barat ↑

1 🥾 🥾

TAMAN NASIONAL BALI BARAT

A B2 **ℹ** To enter, visitors must apply for a permit at the Park Headquarters, Jalan Raya Gilimanuk, Cekik, (0365) 610 60 **⏱** 7:30am–5pm daily

The far west of Bali is occupied by the spectacular Taman Nasional Bali Barat (West Bali National Park), administered by the Indonesian Forestry Service. This wildlife reserve, established by the Dutch in 1941, is bordered by a large area of protected land. The reserve aims to safeguard Bali's remaining wilderness and provides sanctuary for some threatened species.

Here you can hike through thick rainforests, explore open, dry savannas and coastal mangrove swamps, and snorkel around Menjangan Island. The park is home to more than 200 plant species and over 300 different species of animals and birds, most particularly the rare and endangered Bali starling. Other protected fauna include the scaly anteater, the black giant squirrel, the Malayan porcupine and the marbled cat. Permits are required for anyone who wants to enter the park and visitors must be accompanied by an official guide. Only travel on foot is allowed.

THE BALI STARLING

The Bali starling (*Leucopsar rothschildi*) is the only surviving bird endemic to Bali and one of the world's most endangered bird species. Since 2005 efforts have been made to raise their numbers. The conservation project at West Bali National Park aims to save the species, by breeding the birds in captivity before releasing them to the wild.

↑ The sea around Menjangan Island, rich in fish and coral

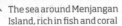

Nature Walk

▽ A short trek with a guide from the park headquarters passes by rivers and through rainforest. Along the route are several forest shrines.

Grasslands

Fertile grasslands stretch out towards the sea near the quiet beach of Pantai Gondol. A fishery research project is located here.

Highlights

Sambar Deer

△ The forested mountain slopes are the habitat of Sambar deer, which roam freely in the park.

Balinese Sapi

These local cattle, descended from the now rare wild banteng, have been domesticated for heavy work in the rice fields.

Mangroves

△ Mangrove roots protect the coast from erosion; the wetlands are home to fish, mudskippers and crabs.

↑ Pasar Anyar market stalls selling fresh produce and flowers

SINGARAJA

🏠D1 🚌 Terminal on Jalan Surapati, Jalan Ahmad Yani & at Sangket 🛈 Jalan Veteran 2; (0361) 25 141

North Bali's main commercial centre, Singaraja was the administrative capital of Bali in colonial times and is Bali's second largest city after Denpasar. With its charming waterfront and Dutch colonial buildings, this historic royal city is a pleasant place to stroll.

① Chinese Temple

🏠 Jalan Erlanga 65
📞 (0368) 263 32

With its classical red roof titles, decorated with tablets in gold calligraphy, this temple indicates the strong presence and influence of the Chinese trading community in this part of Singaraja.

② Pasar Anyar Markets

🏠 Jalan Dipenogoro and Jalan Gajah Mada
🕐 24 hours daily

There are two markets in Singaraja. The market at Jalan Dipenogoro has a wealth of busy stalls selling fresh fruit, vegetables, fish, meat, flowers and utensils, while the smaller one on Jalan Gajah Mada sells all manner of handicrafts and souvenirs, and becomes particularly lively after sundown when the temperature cools.

③ Pura Jagat Natha

🏠 Jalan Pramuka

Singaraja's main temple is a large complex of buildings covered in fine stone carvings. Evening *gamelan* rehearsals take place in one of the courtyards. Entry is with a donation.

④ Puri Singaraja Royal Palace

🏠 Jalan Mayor Metra
📞 (0362) 229 74
🕐 4–6pm daily

Often also referred to as the Puri Agung or Puri Gede, this royal palace, originally built in

↑ Traditional Balinese carved timber veranda, in Puri Singaraja palace

Did You Know?

Singaraja is one of the few places in Bali where Dutch, Chinese and Islamic influences can be seen.

the early 17th century, was the main residence of the rulers of the kingdom of Bululeng. It was destroyed by the colonial Dutch invaders and then rebuilt in the early 19th century. The palace is a fascinating network of interlocking open courtyards and traditional Balinese architecture of single-storey houses, shrines and temples. It is open for guided tours.

⑤

Puri Sinar Nadiputra

Jalan Veteran, next to Gedong Kertya
Mon-Thu & Sat

Housed in a former palace is the Puri Sinar Nadiputra weaving factory, where you can observe the textile-making process and buy the products. Silk and cotton *ikat* cloth is sold in the adjacent shop.

⑥

Independence Monument

Jalan Pelabuhan Buleleng

At the old harbour and waterfront is the striking Independence Monument showing the freedom fighter Yudha Mandala Tama pointing out to sea. He was killed by gunfire from a Dutch warship when he replaced the Dutch flag with the Indonesian flag early in the struggle for independence. The harbour and its pier is one of the most picturesque parts of town.

⑦

Gedong Kertya

Jalan Veteran 20 & 22
(0362) 22 645 7am-2:30pm Mon-Thu, 7am-noon Fri

Founded by the Dutch in 1928, Gedong Kertya is a museum displaying a vast collection of old Balinese *lontar* books and manuscripts, the only *lontar* museum in the world. The books cover subjects such as history, literature, mythology and religion. There are also some even older works in the form of inscribed copper plates called *prasati*, which feature traditional stories.

⑧

Nagasephaha

8 km (5 miles) south of Singaraja

The village of Nagasepaha is famous for its tradition of glass painting. Its initiator was a local puppet master,

LONTAR

An iconic example of Bali's heritage, *lontar* books are made from fan-shaped *rontal* palm leaves. The leaves are dried, soaked in water, cleaned, steamed, dried again and then flattened, dyed and cut into strips. These are inscribed with words and illustrations using a very sharp stylus and are then coated with a black stain, which is wiped off, making the marks legible.

Jero Dalang Diah, who used to carve the characters for his stories out of buffalo or cow leather before painting them. In 1950, he was inspired by a Japanese glass painting and began to paint on glass, using images from Balinese *wayang* stories. Today, his descendants and several neighbours in the village practise this artform and sell their glass paintings.

③ Ⓜ

PURA MEDUWE KARANG

🅰E1 🅾 Jalan Raya Air Sanih, Kubutambahan
🚌 From Singaraja 🕐 8am–5pm daily

The large "temple of the landowner", built in the late 19th century and dedicated to agricultural spirits, is notable for its statuary and carved panels.

Considered one of Bali's principle temples due to its size, Pura Meduwe Karang has a flowery style of decoration characteristic of the north of the island. There are successive split gates and a set of two symmetrical *gedong*, or pavilions. The highest point is the towering, elaborately decorated Betara Luhur Ing Angkasa shrine. The most famous and unusual sculpted panel is on the base of the main plinth in the inner enclosure. It is a highly stylised depiciton of a man riding a bicycle with a lotus flower serving as the back wheel.

Did You Know?

Meduwe Karang is the god of protection of agricultural land.

The long pavilion at the side of the forecourt is used for gatherings during festival celebrations.

→
Plan of the layout of Pura Meduwe Karang

The grand parade of 34 stone figures lined up on the entrance terrace are all characters from the Indian *Ramayana* epic.

Terraces at different levels are linked by steps.

←
Stone sculptures of figures from the ancient Indian *Ramayana* poem

At each level of the temple the ascent to the main shrine passes through a candi bentar (split gate) decorated with relief carvings.

A westerner on a bicycle with a lotus flower serving as the back wheel is depicted on the side of the main shrine. He is believed to be the Dutch artist W O J Nieuwenkamp, who came here in 1904, and is believed to have brought the first bicycle to Bali

The impressive Betara Luhur Ing Angkasa main shrine honours the "Lord possessing the ground". Offerings are also made at the shrine to the sun-god Surya and to Mother Earth for fertility of the agricultural land.

Sculptures illustrating subjects from Balinese legend decorate the walls around the central courtyard.

Reliefs adorning the courtyard walls show people and scenes from everyday life.

Elaborately carved paduraksa (stone posts)

Ornate columns in place of walls distinguish this temple from others in Bali.

The walls of the courtyard are reinforced at intervals by pillars topped with carved decorations.

1

2

3

[1] The temple entrance has three rows of *Ramayana* statues.

[2] At the entrance are stone figures such as this statue of the guardian angel of the temple.

[3] This carving of a man riding a bicycle is thought to be of Dutch artist W O J Nieuwenkamp, the first western artist to visit Bali in 1904.

④ ✍️

PURA TAMAN AYUN

🅰D3 🏠Mengwi 📞(0361) 756 176
🚌From Denpasar 🕘9am–4pm daily
🚫Some sections closed to public
except during festivals

The Taman Ayun ("Vast Garden")
temple, in its moated setting,
symbolizes the Hindu world set
in the cosmic sea. It features
beautiful traditional architecture
set in expansive gardens with
lotus and fish ponds.

Located on an axis connecting the mountains
with the sea, Pura Taman Ayun is thought to
ensure the harmonious circulation of water from the
mountains of Bali to the rice fields, then to the sea, and
back to the mountains. The *meru* towers represent the
mountains, residence of the gods.

Originally established around 1634 by the then-ruler of the
Mengwi kingdom, the temple was restored in 1937. In it are
the ancestral shrines of the former ruling Mengwi family and
their dependants, as well as shrines dedicated to particular
mountains, such as Gunung Batur, Gunung Agung and
Gunung Batukaru, to the sea and to agricultural deities.

↑ *Meru* towers, serving as
shrines to the deities of
Bali's mountains

→
Traditional stone
carved statue on the
wooden pavilion in
Pura Taman Ayun

Did You Know?

The brick walls delineating the main temple areas are built the traditional way, without mortar.

↑ Kori Agung, the main gate to Pura Taman Ayun; detail of a statue of Sai *(inset)*, a guardian figure on the lintel of the gate

EXPERIENCE MORE

⑤ 🏃 🍴 🏪 🛍️

Pura Tanah Lot

📍D4 🏠 Tanah Lot 🚌 From Denpasar & Kediri
ℹ️ Tabanan; (0361) 811 602
🕐 Daily

One of Bali's most heavily promoted landmarks, Pura Tanah Lot is a temple set dramatically on a small island about 100 m (110 yards) off the coast. It can get very crowded, and it is best to arrive well before sunset, when there are not too many visitors around. As the sun goes down, the shrines make a magnificent silhouette against a glowing horizon – a memorable sight despite the throngs of visitors at this time. The many handicraft, souvenir and refreshment stalls at Tanah Lot are a major source of income for the region's women and children.

The islet – a promontory until the beginning of the 20th century – is accessible on foot at low tide, but only Balinese Hindus may go inside the temple. It is being eroded by the onslaught of the sea. The cliffs around the island have been carefully reinforced with concrete, and tripods have been sunk into the sea to act as breakwaters.

As its name suggests, the temple is situated at the meeting point of land *(tanah)* and sea *(lot)*. The part that faces the sea is dedicated to the Balinese goddess of the sea, Betara Tengah Segara, while the landward side is thought to be the seat of the gods from Gunung Batukaru *(p160)*. The temple is associated with the saint Dang Hyang Nirartha. He is said to have advised its construction in order to protect Bali against scourges and epidemics; these destructive forces were thought to originate from the sea.

Along the nearby coast, numerous temples and shrines have been built to protect Tanah Lot. They include Pura Pekendungan, Pura Jero Kandang, Pura Galuh and Pura Batu Bolong.

The last of these, a short distance north of Pura Tanah Lot and rarely visited by tourists, is at the end of a rocky promontory that leaps seaward to form a natural bridge over the waters of the Indian Ocean.

---

⑥ 🛍️

Kapal

📍E3 🚌 From Kediri and Denpasar ℹ️ Tabanan; (0361) 811 602

The most conspicuous feature of Kapal is hundreds of shops selling ready-made temple shrines and somewhat kitsch cement statues. There is also some attractive earthenware.

In a quiet street leading off the main road is **Pura Sada**, the temple of origin of the royal house of Mengwi. A donation is expected to enter. Damaged during an earthquake in 1917, it was rebuilt in the 1960s by a team of Indonesian archaeologists,

← The temple at Tanah Lot, where land and sea meet; one of its guard statues *(inset)*

rows of mini-shrines in the temple yard are said to commemorate the crew of a ship that sank while transporting to Bali the sacred effigy of a Majapahit king.

Pura Sada

🏛 Banjar Pemebetan, near Banjar Celuk, Kapal ⏰ Daily

---

7 🏛
Pejaten

🅰 D3 🚌 From Denpasar & Tanah Lot 🚹 Tabanan; (0361) 811 602

The village of Pejaten is home to a considerable cottage industry that produces terracotta roof tiles, earthenware, pots with coloured glazes, and other decorative objects often attractively naive in character. It is a good place to browse and bargain.

About 3 km (2 miles) northeast of Pejaten is the village of Kediri, where an ornate white statue marks its centre. Kediri is important locally for its cattle market and colourful

based on the 17th-century original. The most interesting part is the 11-tier stone *meru* built in the style of a Javanese *candi*. Such towers are known as *prasada*, and are very rare in Bali. This example is a reminder of the kings' claimed descent from the Majapahit *(p54)*. The tall, 16-m- (53-ft-) high phallic form emphasizes its dedication to the Hindu god Shiva. Affixed to the sides of the tower are images of the eight lords of the compass directions. Vishnu and Brahma with Shiva, the deities of the Hindu Trimurti (triad), are portrayed on the eastern side. On the lower base of the tower are represented the seven seers of the Hindu-Balinese cosmos. The *candi bentar* (split gate) is decorated with sets of Boma (guardian spirit) heads on the front and back; these are split like the gate itself. The closely packed

fabrics. The road from here south to Tanah Lot crosses enchanting rural landscapes.

8
Krambitan

🅰 D3 🚌 From Tabanan 🚹 Tabanan; (0361) 811 602

The small town of Krambitan was an old agrarian kingdom until the turn of the 20th century. It still has a village-like atmosphere and some old architecture. Krambitan is an important repository of Balinese classical culture.

There are two very interesting 17th-century royal palaces, Puri Anyar and Puri Agung Wisata. It's possible, for a donation, to look around the lovely buildings and pavilions. Occasionally, "royal parties" of Balinese dance take place, complete with torches and *tektekan*, a form of gamelan music in which *cenceng* (cymbals) are augmented by bamboo sticks or wooden cowbells.

Klating Beach, on the coast 6 km (4 miles) south of Krambitan, is an unspoiled black-sand beach with some simple *losmen* (guesthouses) available nearby.

TAKE A PEEK AT PALACE LIFE

When the royal estates of Puri Anyar were confiscated under the 1961 law of Land Reform, the enterprising family turned their hands to hospitality, hosting fabulous banquets for visiting politicians, ambassadors and celebrities. If the gates are open, you're welcome to have a look around the vast, antique-filled compound; if you're very lucky, the prince himself will give you a tour.

Tabanan

D3 From Denpasar
Jalan Gunung Agung;
(0361) 811 602

This is a bustling commercial town. The interesting, if somewhat rundown **Museum Subak** has mock-ups of the *subak* irrigation systems of Bali, whereby associations are formed by owners of land irrigated by a common water source. Traditional farming implements are also displayed. Entry is with a donation.

Surabrata, also called Balian Beach, 30 km (19 miles) west of Tabanan, is charming. It has a fishing village set by a cliff, and a small river called "Sacred River" – a name intended to appeal to visitors. The surfing is good and basic accommodation is available.

Museum Subak

Jalan Gatot Subroto,
Sanggulan (0361) 810 315
Daily Public holidays

Bali Butterfly Park

D3 Jalan Batukau,
Sandan Wanasari (0361)
894 0595 8am-5pm daily

Located in the Tabanan regency, Bali Butterfly Park (Taman Kupu-Kupu Bali) is Indonesia's largest butterfly enclosure – an educational conservation area for the preservation of butterflies and insects. A visit to the park is an opportunity to encounter rare and endemic species of butterflies, which are best seen on dry days in the early mornings when they are at their most active. The park promotes the study, breeding and preservation of the 15 known species of butterfly that thrive in Indonesia's tropics, as well as various other insects and arachnids, in extensive and informative displays. Visitors have the opportunity to see the many stages of metamorphosis, from egg, larvae and pupae to cocoon and newly emerged butterflies drying their wings. Colourful and protected specimens include the common birdwing *(Troides helena)*, the Bali peacock *(Papilio peranthus)* and the paradise birdwing *(Ornithoptera paradisea)*.

Marga

E3 From Denpasar &
Mengwi Tabanan; (0361)
811 602

The village of Marga was the site of a battle between the Dutch and the Balinese guerrillas in 1946. On the western side of the village is the Margarana Monument. Besides the graves of the 95 guerrillas who died in the battle of Marga, the garden contains monuments to 1,372 heroes of the War of Independence in the 1940s. The graves do not resemble Christian, Muslim or even Hindu graves: they are small, *meru*-shaped structures reminiscent of the ancient temples from the Javanese empire of Majapahit *(p54)*.

The central monument, not to be mistaken for a Balinese *meru* shrine, is designed to symbolize the day of the proclamation of independence, 17 August 1945. The four steps and five small pillars at its foot represent the year (45); the eight tiers of its roof give the month (August); and the height of 17 m (56 ft) gives the day (17). A statue of Gusti Ngurah Rai *(p57)* completes the scene.

Blayu

E3 From Denpasar &
Kediri Tabanan; (0361)
811 602

Blayu, like nearby Mambal, is a scenic village on a road lined with beautiful *kori* house gates typical of the area. Near the village is the monkey forest of Alas Kedaton. In the temple, **Pura Alas Kedaton**, is an ancient statue of Ganesha, the Hindu god of knowledge.

Pura Alas Kedaton

Daily

BATTLE OF MARGA

In 1946, after Japan surrendered at the end of World War II, the Dutch strove to re-establish their colonial authority in Bali. Local nationalists led a guerrilla war against them. On 20 November 1946, 95 Balinese fighters commanded by Gusti Ngurah Rai were trapped by Dutch troops near Marga. Surrounded on the ground and strafed from the air, they fought to the last, in a modern repeat of the ritual *puputan* (mass suicide). The Margarana Monument pays tribute to their sacrifice.

Avenue leading to the temple in the Sangeh Monkey Forest; a long-tailed macaque *(inset)* ↑

⑬ 🖥️ 🛍️
Sangeh

🅰️ E3 🚌 **From Denpasar**
ℹ️ **Tabanan; (0361) 811 602**

The village of Sangeh is home to an inspiring community rural tourism project. Local guides lead visitors on a gentle trek through a forest of fruit trees, past small farms, to Tirta Taman Mumbul, where huge trees shade an emerald-green lake, inhabited by giant koi fish. An enchanting water temple, Pura Ulun Mumbul, appears to float upon the lake, while a lofty banyan tree shelters a small statue of an elderly water-bearer. Legend has it that the old woman stopped for a rest at this spot, took pity on the dry land and watered the shrivelled-up plants; miraculously, the water continued to pour from her small jar to form the lake that we see today.

On the opposite side of the road is Pancoran Solas, a holy spring, which is channelled into a shallow bathing pool through eleven waterspouts guarded by statues of eleven Hindu gods. The Balinese come here to receive a ritual blessing while bathing in the purifying waters. Close by is Pondok Jaka, an old Balinese compound and farm, featuring traditional grass-roofed houses with bamboo walls, rendered with a mixture of mud and rice husks.

---

⑭ 🖥️ 🛍️
Sangeh Monkey Forest

🅰️ E3 🚌 **From Denpasar**
ℹ️ **Tabanan; (0361) 811 602**

Monkeys are found in many gorges and mountains in Bali, and a good place to see them is the monkey forest of Sangeh, next to the village, where the palahlar trees (*Dipterocarpus trinervis*, often mistakenly described as nutmeg trees) are up to 30–40 m (100–130 ft) high. Monkeys can be seen around a small temple, **Pura Bukit Sari**, deep in the woods but signposted on the main road. The monkeys are considered sacred, a tradition deriving from the Hindu *Ramayana* epic, in which Prince Rama allied himself with the monkey kings Subali and Hanoman to attack the evil king Rawana.

The monkeys – from a colony of around 700 grey long-tailed macaques – should be approached with caution. It is not advisable to get too friendly or the situation can quickly get out of hand. The monkeys may try to climb up on visitors' shoulders, and will not get down unless given something to eat, and while they are generally gentle, sociable creatures, panicky or brusque movements can provoke them to bite. The animals may even take spectacles, phones or money, in which case a *pawang* (monkey tamer) will retrieve the stolen object using a banana as an incentive.

Pura Bukit Sari
⊗ 🏠 Sangeh ⏰ Daily

15

Yeh Panas

D3 **Penatahan, near Penebel** **(0361) 262 356** **From Denpasar & Tabanan** **6am–8pm daily**

It is worthwhile dropping by the Yeh Panas hot springs on the road to Gunung Batukaru from Tabanan or Penebel. The main hot springs have been turned into a spa, which also has a hotel; those which are open to the public are clearly indicated by signs. There is also a spring temple here.

Hot springs are also to be found in the village of Angsri near Apuan. They are in a pleasant, natural setting, but have no modern facilities.

16

Gunung Batukaru

D2 **From Denpasar & Tabanan** **Tabanan; (0361) 811 602**

Gunung Batukaru (also known as Batukau) is the second-highest peak in Bali after Gunung Agung. On its slopes is the last remaining true rainforest on the island. The mountain is much revered as the source of irrigation water for areas its south and west.

The temple of Pura Luhur Batukaru, with its shrine dedicated to the Lord of Gunung Batukaru and the goddess of nearby Lake Tamblingan (p165), is located among the lofty trees at its foot. There is a constant stream of worshippers performing rites or requesting holy water from the temple priests.

The charm of the temple's setting lies in a blend of artifice and nature: the spires of its *meru* shrines and other dark-thatched pavilions appear to have sprouted up among the greens of the trees, foliage and mosses. The name given to the central deity of the temple is Sang Hyang Tumuwuh, "The Ultimate Plant Grower".

To the east of Pura Luhur Batukaru on the Baturiti road are the famous rice terraces of Jatiluwih. Rice granaries line the road in the local villages. Other beautiful rice terraces can be seen in Pacung, at the turn-off to Jatiluwih and Batukaru.

17

Pura Gangga

E3 **On a small road leading through Perean to Apuan and Baturiti** **Tabanan; (0361) 811 602**

On the main highway to Bedugul, Pura Gangga temple is set on the lush banks of a small river. The temple has a seven-tier *meru* with a stone base. It is unusual in that the base is open at the front, rather than entirely closed in the usual fashion. Although the temple is not open to visitors, its atmospheric compound and architectural features can easily be viewed from outside the precincts.

Did You Know?

Pura Gangga is named after the holy river Ganges (Gangga) in India.

18

Perancak

B2 **Negara; (0365) 41 060**

The quiet Muslim village of Perancak, settled by migrating Madurese islanders, has a mosque with a tiered roof in the traditional Indonesian style and a tranquil, black-sand beach. The Madurese introduced their unique fishing boat designs to the area. Hidden up the Perancak river estuary, 10 km (6 miles) from Negara, you will find a "secret fleet" – a glittering armada of dozens of large, fully decked, high-prowed, traditional wooden vessels, known as *selerek*. Each boat

is abundantly decorated with Hindu and Muslim iconography, multi-hued carvings and sculptures, crows' nests shaped like mythical winged chariots, flags and bunting, beads and mirrors. More of these colourful boats can be seen at the nearby atmospheric port of Pengambengan, where "dangdut" music blares from the dockside. Dangdut is an amalgamation of ethnic ensemble music combining Malay and Western elements together with Indian film music and urban Arab pop.

Negara

A B2 **🚌** From Denpasar & Gilimanuk **ℹ** Jalan Ngurah Rai; (0365) 41 060

The real charm of Negara lies in the Bugis origin of its urban core. On both sides of the Ijo Gading River, south of the central bridge on Jalan Gatot Subroto, is the Bugis community of Loloan. A walk on its streets evokes the atmosphere of Sulawesi, from where many early Bugis migrants originated. Wooden houses with elaborately carved balconies line the streets. The most beautiful are at the end of Jalan Gunung Agung and on nearby Jalan Puncak Jaya. Loloan has several traditional *pesantren* (Islamic boarding schools).

Negara is also known for its *jegog*, gamelan orchestras playing huge bamboo instruments, and for the *makepung*, a sport which was introduced to West Bali by Madurese migrants from East Java. It is a race between two-wheeled chariots drawn by a pair of water buffaloes. The races, featuring Bali's

←

Gunung Batukaru viewed from rice fields near Pupuan

sleekest, most handsome buffaloes and most daring jockeys, are staged every year to please the god of the harvest.

A small road 4 km (2 miles) west of Negara leads to the quiet beach of Rening, 8 km (5 miles) away. From the nearby Cape Rening there is a beautiful sunset view over the mountains of eastern Java.

To the north are two Christian villages: Palasari (Catholic) and Blimbingsari (Protestant). These were established in the 1930s on state land given by the Dutch to Balinese converts to Christianity, who were excluded from their own community. The architecture in both is an interesting mix of Balinese and Dutch-Nordic styles.

> ### THE NEGARA BUFFALO RACES
>
> Held every July to November, the buffalo races see hundreds of pairs of bulls racing against each other at high speed along rice-field tracks. Festooned with strings of bells, silks and decorative harnesses, each pair is hitched to a brightly painted wooden chariot, driven by a perilously balanced standing jockey. Winning teams gain additional points for stylish presentation.

↑ The Pura Rambut Siwi temple, near Medewi Beach

Medewi Beach

A C2 **🚌** From Denpasar **ℹ** Negara; (0365) 41 060

Medewi is a beautiful rocky beach popular with surfers. The long, rolling breakers can be 7 m (23 ft) high. It tends to be quieter than many other surf hotspots due to being a little out of the way. The beach is composed of black sand, over which are scattered small black stones that glitter under the rays of the setting sun. On the horizon is the Javanese coast.

The **Pura Rambut Siwi** temple complex is built on a promontory, 6 km (4 miles) west of the beach. The setting offers a fine panorama over the sea. The main temple was established to venerate the priest Dang Hyang Nirartha, after he cured the local villagers of a deadly illness. There is a single, three-tiered *meru*. A lock of hair *(rambut)*, believed to be the priest's, is kept as a relic in the pavilion shrine. The temple entrance faces the sea and is guarded by a superbly carved statue of the demon queen Rangda. Entry is with a donation. There are other smaller temples in caves along the nearby cliff.

Pura Rambut Siwi

A 6 km (4 miles) west of Medewi Beach **🕑** Daily

↑ A shoal of blue-green Chromis swimming in the reef around Menjangan Island

21 🍴 🖥 🛍

Gilimanuk

🗺 A1 🚌 From Denpasar & Singaraja ⛴ From Ketapang, Java ℹ Negara; (0365) 41 060

Gilimanuk is the ferry port to Java. There are many *warung* here catering for travellers who sometimes have to wait hours for a ferry.

The main architectural feature is an enormous arched "gateway to Bali", topped by four flaming dragons facing in the cardinal directions, around a central throne of heaven.

North of Gilimanuk at Cekik, the **Museum Purbakala** (Archaeological Museum) displays some sarcophagi and Neolithic tools excavated from a nearby funerary site. Some promising archaeological discoveries have been made here showing signs of pre-Bronze Age human settlement in this area. Also in Cekik is the headquarters of the Taman Nasional Bali Barat *(p148)*, the nature reserve covering a substantial area of West Bali.

Museum Purbakala
⊕ ⊛ 🏠 Jalan Raya 📞 (0365) 61 328 🕐 8am–4pm Tue–Sun

22 ⊛ ⊛

Makam Jayaprana

🗺 A1 🏠 Teluk Terima 🚌 From Denpasar & Seririt ℹ Singaraja; (0362) 25 141 🕐 Daily

The Makam Jayaprana (Jayaprana Mausoleum) is also a temple. It is reached by a climb from the road; however, the panoramic view over Gunung Raung in Java, Menjangan Island and Gilimanuk is ample reward for the effort required to get there. The shrine was built on the burial site of Jayaprana, a romantic hero of Balinese folk-lore. According to legend, Jayaprana had married a woman named Layonsari, of such extreme beauty that the Lord of Kalianget decided to get rid of him and marry her. The king pretended that Bugis pirates had landed in Gilimanuk and sent Jayaprana with a body of soldiers to repel them. When they came to their destination the soldiers killed Jayaprana. However, resisting the advances of the king, Layonsari killed herself to rejoin her beloved Jayaprana in death. Today, suitors ask for favours of love

at the grave. It is decorated with statues of Jayaprana and Layonsari.

23 ⊛ ⊛

Menjangan Island

🗺 A1 🚌 To Labuhan Lalang from Denpasar & Seririt ⛴ From Labuhan Lalang ℹ Labuhan Lalang; (0365) 61 060

For those who wish to dive and snorkel in a pristine environment, Menjangan Island is not to be missed. Technically not part of the Taman Nasional Bali Barat *(p148)*, it owes its name to the Java deer *(menjangan)*, which swim across from the mainland. There are eight main diving points around the island, each with its own marine

Did You Know?

Pemuteran is home to the world's largest coral-reef restoration project.

STAY

Mimpi Resort Menjangan

This charming resort on Banyuwedang Bay has a spa, swimming pool, hot-spring pools, patio rooms and villas.

🅰B1 🏠Jalan Mimpi, Batuampar, Gerokgak 🌐mimpi.com/ menjangan

⟨Rp⟩⟨Rp⟩⟨Rp⟩

---

life. The best is perhaps the Anchor Wreck, named for the encrusted anchor on the reef.

Labuhan Lalang, on the bay of Teluk Terima, is Bali's nearest point of access to Menjangan Island. Boat tickets may be bought at the office of the Department of Forestry here. The last boats leave for Menjangan Island at 11am and return at dusk. There is basic accommodation at Labuhan Lalang.

---

24 🍴 ☕

Pemuteran

🅰B1 🚌 ℹ️Singaraja; (0362) 25 141

A coastal resort and fishing village, with plenty of accommodation options, Pemuteran has beautiful coral reefs with a profusion of tropical fish. There are good diving and snorkelling spots, and a turtle sanctuary. It is a convenient place for visitors to Menjangan Island to stay overnight; a boat can be rented here. Some hotels offer early-morning dolphin-spotting excursions.

⟶

Pilgrims on the steps of Pura Pulaki, a Hindu temple near Pemuteran

---

A little west of Pemuteran is the small Banyuwedang Bay. The name is Balinese for "hot springs". There are many springs along this shore, supposedly with curative powers. They are alternately covered and exposed by the tide.

Pura Pulaki, about 5 km (3 miles) east of Pemuteran, is a coastal temple near a point where a mountain ridge plunges abruptly into the sea, almost blocking the coastal passage. It is associated with the Shaivite priest Dang Hyang Nirartha, who is said to have turned the local inhabitants into *gamang* (ghosts). Living around it are mischievous monkeys; they are regarded as holy.

Atlas South Sea Pearl Farm, 10 km (6 miles) east of Pemuteran, conducts tours, including a demonstration of pearl seeding and harvesting. The pearls are made into fine pieces of jewellery and exported worldwide.

Guided tours of the **Hatten Wines Vineyard**, 13 km (8 miles) east of Pemuteran, include a visit to the laboratory and demonstrations of the different stages of wine production, followed by a wine tasting.

Pura Pulaki
⊗ 🏠Banyu Poh ⏰Daily

Atlas South Sea Pearl Farm
⊗ 🏠Penyabangan 🌐atlaspearls.com.au/ pages/pearl-farm-tours

Hatten Wines Vineyard
⊗ 🏠Sanggalangit 🌐hattenwines.com/ vineyards-welcome-center

25

Pantai Gondol

🅰B1 🚗6 km (4 miles) west of Gerokgak, across the field next to the Fisheries Research Project (Perikanan) 🚌 ℹ️Singaraja; (0362) 25 141

The beautiful, serene white-sand Gondol beach is located at the foot of a small promontory, the Gondol Cape. With stunning coral, it is a good, uncrowded spot for snorkelling and diving.

26 🍴 🍺 🛍️

Banjar

🅰️ D1 🚌 To Seririt, then own transport 🅸 Singaraja; (0362) 25141

Set on the coastal plain with the North Bali uplands as a backdrop, Banjar is a town of historic significance. In 1871, when still a semi-independent kingdom run by a Brahman family, it put up strong resistance to Dutch encroachment during the Banjar War. The ruling family was eliminated in one of Bali's first recorded *puputan*, or mass ritual suicide in preference to surrender.

The Brahmans from Banjar are famous for their literary talents. In the 19th century they adapted texts from classical Kawi (Old Javanese) into common Balinese.

Brahma Vihara Arama is a Buddhist monastery built in 1970 by a powerful local Brahman, Bhikku Giri Rakhita, who converted to Theravada Buddhism, the form of Buddhism prevalent in Thailand. Visitors are welcome, but overnight rooms are only available for participants in meditation courses.

Another highlight of Banjar is the **Air Panas** hot spring, popular with both locals and visitors from nearby Lovina. Entry is with a donation. There are three pools; in the highest one the water is hot. Eight carved dragon-heads spurt out greenish-yellow, sulphurous water believed to be therapeutic for complaints of the skin. The hot water is considered sacred by the locals – a temple has been built around the spring, which is set in cool and shady surroundings.

From Banjar it is worth visiting Pedawa, 10 km (6 miles) inland. This remote place is a Bali Aga village. It was one of the villages which rebelled against the Javanese occupation of 1343, and has retained Hindu cultural features dating from before

Bathers at the Air Panas hot spring in Banjar; detail of dragon-head spouts *(inset)*

> The forest by Lake Tamblingan resounds with birdsong, and you may spot babblers, woodpeckers, ground thrushes and malkohas.

that time. Indeed, the Hindu triad of Brahma-Vishnu-Shiva was unknown here until recently. While the Balinese generally build a range of shrines for gods and ancestors behind their houses, the people of Pedawa build a single bamboo structure.

There are two routes from Banjar to Pedawa: both run through stunning mountain and plantation landscapes.

In Sidatapa, another Bali Aga village 8 km (5 miles) from Banjar, some interesting old houses made of bamboo still remain. This is one of the oldest villages in North Bali, dating to the first century AD.

Brahma Vihara Arama
♿ 🕐 🅰️ Between Banjar and Pedawa 🕐 8am–6pm daily 🌐 brahmaviharaarama.com

Air Panas
🕐 8am–6pm daily

Munduk

🅐D2 🚌 From Singaraja & Seririt 🛈 Singaraja; (0362) 25 141

Munduk is a highland village amid plantations of coffee and cloves. It is set on a high ridge near the volcanic lakes of Tamblingan, Buyan and Bratan. In the area there are still a few resthouses from the 1920s, built in a mixed Dutch Colonial-Chinese style. In the village it is possible to visit the workshop of I Made Trip, Bali's most famous maker of bamboo instruments.

Munduk is an ideal base for exploring on rented bicycles, for mountain walks to Pedawa, for rice-field walks to Uma Jero, or for a tour of Lake Tamblingan and Lake Bratan. There are several waterfalls in the area – the most impressive are 30 m (100 ft) high, and can be found 1 km (half a mile) along the road eastwards to Bedugul. The path down to the waterfall is dense with clove and coffee trees.

Pupuan

🅐D2 🚌 From Denpasar & Singaraja 🛈 Tabanan; (0361) 811 602

Situated in the rainiest part of the whole island, Pupuan is Bali's vegetable-growing centre. The area around it is cool and mountainous. The road from Seririt to Antosari travels through some of Bali's most beautiful landscape, with excellent coastal views. It climbs steeply via Busungbiu, Pupuan and through a forested pass 790 m (2,600 ft) high into lush spice-growing countryside. It then winds down to Blimbing and Bajra before passing rice terraces, with rice barns along the road. The road southwest towards Pekutatan passes a coffee plantation area, and at one

↑ Harvesting hydrangeas in the fields surrounding Lake Tamblingan

point is arched by the roots of a huge bunutan tree. Dlimbing, 12 km (7 miles) to the south, has the nearest accommodation, panoramic views and a restaurant.

Lake Tamblingan

🅐D2 🚌 From Bedugul or Munduk

A scenic road follows the rim of the massive Catur Caldera overlooking the northern shores of Lake Buyan and

↑ A road through the roots of a huge bunutan tree near Pupuan

> 💬 INSIDER TIP
> **Walking**
>
> Avoid rainy season (Oct–Apr) when the trails around the lake are slippery. The forest paths are narrow and the undergrowth can be up to 2 m (7 ft) high. In dry season it is easy to negotiate the route.

Lake Tamblingan. Rustic bamboo viewing stations line the road, and the views are awe-inspiring. For an experience of being close to nature, trek through the ancient rainforest, which is accessed via a flight of stone steps on the shoulder of land between the two lakes. The forest resounds with birdsong, and you may spot babblers, woodpeckers, ground thrushes and malkohas. The pathways lead to a clearing beside Lake Tamblingan, next to Pura Tahun, a temple with an 11-roofed *meru*. Motorboats and watersports are forbidden, but you may arrange for a boatman to row you across the lake in a *pedau akit*, a traditional double canoe, to the tiny village of Munduk Tamblingan, where you will find Pura Gubug (the Farmers' Temple), dedicated to the lake goddess.

30 🍴 🛍️

Lake Buyan

🅰️ D2 🚌 From Singaraja
ℹ️ Singaraja; (0362) 25 141

There are great views over the lake from the mountain road – dense forest scrub vanishes at the shoreline into the water. Boats can be hired from local fishermen and treks organized to a cave on the slopes of Gunung Lesong, to Gesing or to Munduk.

31 🍴 🍽️ 🛍️

Lake Bratan and Bedugul

🅰️ E2 🚌 From Singaraja & Denpasar ℹ️ Tabanan; (0361) 811 602

Lake Bratan offers a variety of water activities such as para-sailing and water-skiing. Visitors can hire boats, and there are guides for treks to peaks such as Gunung Catur and Gunung Puncak Manggu. The lake is the setting for the 17th-century Pura Ulun Danu Bratan temple, built on a small island and dedicated to the goddess of the lake, Dewi Danu. There is a small stupa-shaped shrine for Buddhist worshippers, with statues of Buddhas occupying

niches that mark the four points of the compass. The panorama includes an 11-tiered *meru* located on the shore across a wooden bridge.

The 1.5 sq km (0.6 sq m) **Bali Botanic Garden** contains 320 species of orchids, a fern garden, a herbarium and a collection of plants used for making *jamu* (traditional medicines). Also in the botanic garden is the Bali Treetop Adventure Park.

North of Lake Bratan, the well-kept Bali Handara Kosaido Country Club has a world-class golf course.

Bali Botanic Garden

🌿🍽️ 🅰️ Kebun Raya, west of Candi Kuning ⏰ Daily 🌐 kebunrayabali.com

32 🍽️ 🍴 🛍️

Lovina

🅰️ D1 🚌 ℹ️ Kalibukbuk; (0362) 41 910

The long stretch of coast encompassing several villages, from Tukadmungga in the east

to Kaliasem in the west, is collectively known as Lovina. The beach resort area has quiet, black-sand coves lined with coconut trees. Outriggers add to the nostalgic charm, and are available for early-morning dolphin-watching excursions. For snorkellers, there are pristine coral reefs.

The tourist facilities of Lovina are on Jalan Binaria, which leads to a modern sculpture of dolphins. From the village of Temukus, it is possible to trek to the Singsing Waterfall.

33

Jagaraga

🅰️ E1 🚌 From Singaraja ℹ️ Singaraja; (0362) 25 141

Jagaraga was the site of a battle in 1849, in which the war hero Patih Jelantik held

Did You Know?

It is thought that the name Lovina is derived from "Lov" and "Ina", meaning "Love Indonesia".

→

The beautiful Gitgit waterfall surrounded by tropical rainforest

the Dutch to a long stand-off before he was defeated. The relationship between the Balinese and the Dutch is reflected in the lively reliefs of the local temple of the dead, **Pura Dalem**. These were carved in the early decades of the 20th century. The subjects include aircraft, ships and a European in a car being held up by an armed man.

The central gate of Pura Beji in Sangsit, 4 km (3 miles) northwest of Jagaraga, is famous for its ornamentation. Garudas (mythical birds) are carved half in the round, half in low relief. The nearby Pura Dalem has some grim depictions of the tortures in hell inflicted on those who infringe moral rules.

The country around Sawan, 4 km (3 miles) south of Jagaraga, is said to produce some of Bali's best rice. There are impressive river gorges in the area. Sawan is also known for its northern dance and music tradition.

About 12 km (8 miles) east of Sangsit, Air Sanih is a small beach resort named after a

spring feeding a natural pool, which is great for swimming. There is a beach restaurant and basic accommodation.

Pura Dalem
🚗🏍️ 🅰️ Jagaraga 🕐 Daily

34 🍴 🛍️

Gitgit

🅰️ D1 🚌 From Singaraja & Bedugul 🛈 Singaraja; (0362) 25 141

This village is the location of an impressive waterfall, 45 m (149 ft) high, about 400 m (450 yds) from the main road and surrounded by lush vegetation. Another waterfall, 1 km (half a mile) up the hill, is not quite as high, but there are fewer visitors there.

Pegayaman, just north of Gitgit, maintains 17th-century Javanese traditions. On the

←

Pura Ulun Danu Bratan water temple on the shore of Lake Bratan

Prophet's birthday, Muslim villagers parade a *tumpeng* (mountain-shaped offering).

35

Tejakula

🅰️ F1 🚌 From Singaraja 🛈 Singaraja; (0362) 25 141

The old village of Tejakula is famous for its silver jewellery and its ancient *wayang wong* traditional dance. This eastern part of the regency of Buleleng is one of the most unspoiled areas of Bali. At Tejakula itself there are some quiet black beaches and idyllic coconut groves.

Nearby are several Bali Aga villages. One of them, Sembiran (a short way up the mountain road west of Tejakula), has the charac-teristic stone-paved roads, some megalithic remains and good views down to the north coast.

A pleasant walk upriver, 8 km (5 miles) east of Tejakula, leads to the mighty Yeh Mempeh (Flying Water) waterfall.

LOMBOK

The Sasaks are the indigenous people of Lombok. Numbering about three million, they are thought to be descended from a hill tribe of North India and Myanmar. The minority Balinese population, about 100,000, live mostly near the west coast.

Lombok's identity has been formed by two major influences. Javanese arrivals in the 14th century brought Islam and Middle-Eastern influences, while the Balinese Hindus, who were the colonial masters of the island from the 16th century until the 1890s, have been an important presence. These groups give the island a rich heritage of dialects and languages, traditional dance, music, rituals and crafts.

Lombok appeals to visitors for its natural beauty more than for its architectural heritage. The island's varied geography provides ideal conditions for trekking, surfing and windsurfing, diving, snorkelling and game fishing. However, like Bali, Lombok sits on the so-called "ring of fire", and devastating earthquakes in July and August 2018 killed over 500 and caused inestimable damage. Thousands of tourists on the Gili Islands and Mount Rinjani had to be evacuated.

LOMBOK

Must Sees
1. Taman Nasional Gunung Rinjani
2. Gili Islands
3. Mataram

Experience More
4. Lembar
5. Sweta
6. Narmada
7. Senggigi
8. Tanjung
9. Segenter
10. Sembalun
11. Bayan Beleq Mosque
12. Sapit
13. Senaru
14. Labuhan Lombok
15. Pringgasela
16. Tetebatu
17. Rembitan and Sade
18. Gerupuk
19. Sukarara
20. Penujak
21. Kuta
22. Tanjung Aan Beach
23. Mawun Beach
24. Bangko Bangko
25. Selong Blanak
26. Tanjung Luar
27. Banyumulek
28. Southwestern Gili Islands

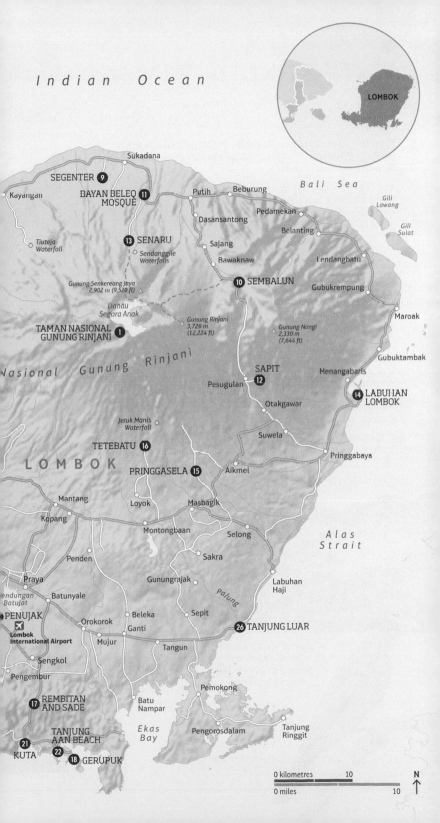

Indian Ocean

Bali Sea

LOMBOK

Sukadana

SEGENTER **9**

Kayangan

BAYAN BELEQ **11**
MOSQUE

Putih

Beburung

Pedamekan

Gili
Lawang

Gili
Sulat

Dasansantong

Belanting

Tiuteja
Waterfall

13 SENARU

Sendanggile
Waterfalls

Sajang

Bawaknaw

Lendangbatu

Gunung Senkereang Jaya
2,902 m (9,520 ft)

10 SEMBALUN

Gubukrempung

Danau
Segara Anak

Gunung Rinjani
3,726 m
(12,224 ft)

Gunung Nangi
2,330 m
(7,644 ft)

Maroak

TAMAN NASIONAL
GUNUNG RINJANI **1**

Gubuktambak

Nasional   Gunung   Rinjani

SAPIT
12

Menangabaris

Pesugulan

14 LABUHAN
LOMBOK

Otakgawar

Jeruk Manis
Waterfall

Suwela

TETEBATU **16**

Pringgabaya

PRINGGASELA **15**

Aikmel

L O M B O K

Mantang

Loyok

Masbagik

Kopang

Montongbaan

Selong

Alas
Strait

Penden

Sakra

Praya

Gunungrajak

endungan
Batujat

Batunyale

PENUJAK

Orokorok

Beleka

Sepit

Labuhan
Haji

Palung

Lombok
International Airport

Ganti

Mujur

Tangun

26 TANJUNG LUAR

Sengkol

Pengembur

Pemokong

17 REMBITAN
AND SADE

Batu
Nampar

TANJUNG
AAN BEACH

Ekas
Bay

Pengorosdalam

Tanjung
Ringgit

21
KUTA

22

18 GERUPUK

0 kilometres   10

0 miles   10

N

1 🏛 🏔

TAMAN NASIONAL GUNUNG RINJANI

🅰C4 🚌 to Anyar, then *bemo* to Senaru; to Aikmel, then *bemo* to Sembalu 🛈 Mataram; (0370) 632 723 or 634 800 🕐 All year 🌐 rinjaninationalpark.com

At 3,726 m (12,224 ft) high, Gunung Rinjani volcano towers over the landscape of Lombok and plays an important role in the religions and folklore of both the Hindus and Sasaks of the island.

The mountain and its satellites form the Taman Nasional Gunung Rinjani (Mount Rinjani National Park), a magnet for experienced trekkers and nature lovers. The main entry points to the park are via Senaru or Sembalun villages. Within Mount Rinjani's huge caldera are the stunning Segara Anak crater lake, the Aik Kalak hot springs and the small active cone of Gunung Baru. Hindus and Sasaks regard the mountain (the second-tallest volcano in Indonesia after Mount Kerinci on Sumatra) as sacred, and make pilgrimages to the summit and lake to leave offerings to the gods and spirits.

↑ Sembalun village in a valley surrounded by Gunung Rinjani and towering mountains

💬 INSIDER TIP
Trekking

Guides are mandatory. The easiest and safest way to organize a visit is through a trekking agency in Mataram, Senggigi or Senaru (prices include return transport). Typically, a trek to the crater rim takes two days and one night. The longer and more strenuous ascent to the summit is usually part of a three- to four-day trek. June to August are the best months as they are the driest. Take warm clothing as it can be extremely cold at the rim and summit.

←
The black-naped Oriole, with yellow and black plumage, can be seen in the park

↑ Gunung Baru in the blue-green waters of Lake Segara Anak in the crater rim; trekking to Mount Rinjani *(inset)* from Sembalun

② 🍴 🖥

GILI ISLANDS

🗺 A–B4 🚌 From Senggigi & Mataram to Bangsal 🚢 From Bangsal
or from Benoa Harbour, Sanur and Amed in Bali ℹ Mataram;
0370 632 723 or 634

Lying off the northwest coast of Lombok, the three small islands
known as the Gili Islands form some of Lombok's most spectacular
natural beauty and are a major tourist destination. Especially popular
with divers, the waters around the islands teem with tropical marine
life and have good visibility all year round.

These idyllic islands were "discovered" by
backpackers in the 1980s, who fell in love with
the crystal-clear waters, full of all manner of
colourful marine life, and the pure white-sand
beaches. Simple bungalows with generator-
supplied electricity soon sprang up to cater to
a crowd eager to get off the beaten track. The
popularity of the islands has been growing
steadily since 2005 when the first direct fastboat service was introduced, cutting travel
time from Bali by more than half. Since
then, the development of upmarket hotels,
restaurants and dive centres has taken
place at a rapid rate.

The Lombok earthquakes in July and
August 2018 struck the Gili Islands, wreaking
significant structural damage and temporarily
halting tourism. However, hotel, restaurant,
and dive-centre owners were quick to repair
and rebuild, and the Gili Islands are open for
business once again.

Motorized transport is banned from all three
islands. Transport comprises horse-drawn
carts called *cidomos*, or bicycles which can
be hired by the hour or by the day.

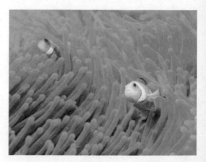

↑ Orange-and-white striped clownfish
in the waters off the Gili islands

←

Aerial
view of the
coastline of Gili
Air; sun rising
behind Mount Rinjani
(inset) seen from Gili Air

🔺 GREAT VIEW
Mandarinfish

If you dive in the Gili Air
Harbour at sunset, you
may get to see the rare
and mesmerizing
Mandarinfish with its
respendent colours –
one of the most beautiful
fish in the ocean.

GILI AIR

Meaning "Little Island of Water", Gili Air is the island closest to the Lombok mainland and the most easily accessed of the three Gilis. While the bars here aren't as loud as on Gili Trawangan, there are still plenty of opportunities to have fun. Most of the development on Gili Air is on the east coast, facing Lombok and the towering Mount Rinjani. From here there are spectacular sunrises, while sunsets behind Mount Agung on Bali are visible from the south and western coasts.

The best beaches are on the south or east side, with clear turquoise waters and soft white sand. Diving facilities abound and there is good snorkelling directly from the shore, particularly from the east and northeast beaches. Gili Air Wall, off the west coast, is a popular dive site, with soft corals gleaming yellow and orange in the sunlight. Here you can see harbour scorpion fish and thousands of glassfish, turtles and, if you look very carefully, tiny pigmy seahorses hiding in the sea fans. In the deeper waters are whitetip reef sharks and schools of larger fish species. Hahn's Reef is a superb training site for beginners. With the right conditions, there are good waves off the south of the island, which attract surfers.

↑ A typical traditional
wooden house in a
village on Gili Air

GILI TRAWANGAN

The furthest from the mainland and the largest of the three Gili islands, yet small enough to walk around in an hour and a half, Gili Trawangan is known as "the party island", yet has a wide range of attractions and facilities to suit a broad spectrum of visitors. Despite the many restaurants and lounge bars lining the shores of its powdery white-sand beaches, it's still possible to find a quiet stretch of beach to enjoy undisturbed, especially on the north and west coasts, while peaceful inland villages provide an experience of authentic rural life. Behind the glitz and glamour, a laidback bohemian atmosphere still prevails.

As well as plenty of backpacker rooms there are many glamorous boutique bungalows, hotels, resorts and private-pool villas. All have been constructed in harmony with the islands' local charms – natural materials and simple elegance are the dominant themes of most developments. There are no high-rise hotels, and definitely no tour buses or fast-food chains, but plenty of dive centres to help visitors explore the islands' fabulous coral reefs.

Gili Trawangan is the island that offers the best choice of activities, including some superb spa facilities, horse-riding stables, sea kayaks for rent, and what claims to be the smallest public cinema in the world, where you can laze on floor cushions and watch newly released movies. There is good snorkelling just off the shore. Strong currents are sometimes a bother, however, especially in the strait with neighbouring Gili Meno. Further out are vast gardens of coral, regarded as one of the best dive spots in Lombok, particularly Shark Point to the east of the island, which is home to a huge number of fish, whitetip reef sharks and green and hawksbill turtles. The hill in the south of the island is a great lookout from which to enjoy the spectacular sunset views across the ocean to Bali; or in the mornings, the brilliant sunrise over Mount Rinjani on Lombok.

↑ Open-sided beach hut on Gili Trawangan, a tropical paradise

---

💬 **INSIDER TIP**
Snorkelling

Masks, snorkels and fins can easily be hired. Wearing rubber shoes can make it easier to get into the water. Currents can cause you to drift so you will need to walk back to where you started. Snorkelling trips in glass-bottomed boats can be arranged on Gili Trawangan along the main strip. A highlight of snorkelling here is that you are very likely to see green and hawksbill turtles.

→
Visitors cycling on rented bikes in palm forest on Gili Meno, the smallest of the islands

GILI MENO

Positioned in the middle, Gili Meno is the smallest of the three Gili Islands. It also has the lowest population – just a few hundred residents. Gili Meno is not as developed as Gili Trawangan or Gili Air, and the pace here is slower. The landscape is flat, with coconut groves inland, and a small and shallow saltwater lake in the west from which the local people harvest meagre supplies of salt during the dry season. The main activities for visitors are yoga, snorkelling and scuba diving. Gili Meno Wall, off the west coast, is a popular dive site, with giant gorgonian fans and many varieties of marine life. Hawksbill and green turtles inhabit the waters around Gili Meno, particularly on the northwest corner, and the reefs just offshore feature outcrops of brilliant blue coral. The best place for snorkelling, meanwhile, is at Blue Coral Point off the northeast coast, where the reef showcases numerous species of coral and colourful fish. At night, divers can witness huge Moray eels, entertaining Spanish dancers, baby cuttlefish and a whole array of crustaceans. At the turtle nursery on Meno, the hatchlings are kept in holding tanks until they are large and healthy enough to be released into the sea. Visitors can take part in this release programme (www.kura kuragilimeno.com). Small donations are welcome.

3 🍴 🖥 🛍

MATARAM

🅰B5 🚌Sweta 🛈Department of Tourism, Art & Culture, Jalan Singosari 2; (0370) 632 723 or (0370) 634 800

Lombok's capital is an urban sprawl of several towns – Mataram, Ampenan and Cakranegara – merged together without a break. The city is characterized by parks and wide, tree-lined streets with buildings which echo traditional Sasak styles.

The city's large, whitewashed, high-roofed houses hark back to Dutch colonial days. Ampenan, to the west, was once Lombok's main port during Dutch colonial times and a vital link in the spice trade. Its old winding streets are lined with shops and restaurants. Some of the buildings show an Art Deco influence. At night, food carts and *warungs* sell inexpensive, tasty food. It also has a colourful Arab quarter. To the east of Ampenan is Mataram, Lombok's administrative centre, with government buildings, mosques and a university. Further east, Cakranegara was the royal capital until a century ago. It is home to many Chinese and Balinese and is today the main business and shopping area, with stores selling gold, textiles and clothing.

↑ The three elegant multi-tiered shrines at Pura Meru

① 🏛 🅼

Museum Negeri

🏠Jalan Panji Tilar Negara 6 ☎(0370) 632 159 🕐8am–3pm Tue–Fri, 8am–3pm Sat & Sun 🚫Public hols

The provincial state museum displays locally made textiles, ceramics, copperwork and woodcarvings, as well as artifacts relating to the islands of West Nusa Tenggara and paintings representing the variety of ethnic cultures.

② 🏛 🅼

Pura Meru

🏠Jalan Selaparang, Cakranegara 🕐Daily

With its three slender *meru* representing the Hindu gods Vishnu, Shiva and Brahma, this is Lombok's largest Hindu temple complex. Built in the early 18th century, it consists of an inner courtyard with many small shrines. The central eleven-tiered *meru* is Shiva's house; the nine-tiered *meru* is Vishnu's home; and the seven-tiered meru is Brahma's abode.

③ 🏛 🅼

Mayura Water Palace

🏠Jalan Selaparang, Cakranegara ☎(0370) 624 442 🕐Daily

This complex was built in 1844 under the Balinese Karangasem dynasty. It

includes the former king's family temple. The centrepiece is a lake, surrounded by a park dotted with shrines and fountains.

SHOP

Lombok Pottery Centre

This arts and crafts complex sells a large variety of handcrafted ceramics. Many are painted with traditional designs, while others are left unpainted, showing their natural colour. Traditionally, no potter's wheel is used. Pots are formed either by hand using "stone and paddle" tools or by coiling lengths of clay.

🏠Jalan Sriwijaya 111A, Mataram ☎(0370) 640 451

↑ Looking over the rooftops and mosque across the city of Mataram

④
Pura Lingsar

🏠 Off Jalan Gora II 🕐 7am–6pm daily

Some 6 km (4 miles) northeast of Mataram in the village of Lingsar, the large Pura Lingsar temple complex was built in 1714 and is nestled in beautiful rice fields. A multi-denominational site, it has a temple for Balinese Hindus (Pura Gaduh), as well as one for Lombok's form of Islam – Wetu Telu. The Wetu Telu temple is noted for its enclosed lily-covered pond and for the holy eels, which can be enticed from hiding (it is considered good luck to feed them) with hard-boiled eggs, which are available for purchase at stalls. Entry to the complex is with a donation.

WETU TELU

A mixture of Hindu, Islamic and indigenous animist beliefs, Wetu Telu is the traditional religion of the Sasak people in Lombok and is officially a sect of Islam. This mystical religion centres on a physical concept of the Holy Trinity: the sun, moon and stars represent heaven, earth and water; the head, body and limbs creativity, sensitivity and control. Unlike most Muslims, followers of Wetu Telu (which means "Three Times") pray three times a day instead of five times, do not fast for the full month of Ramadan and can consume alcohol such as rice wine.

Another more orthodox form of Islam in Lombok is Wetu Lima (meaning "Five Times"). Under Suharto's government in the 1960s, indigenous beliefs such as Wetu Telu were discouraged and today it is mainly practised in the traditional northern heartland of Bayan.

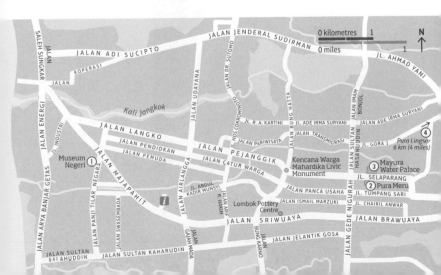

EXPERIENCE MORE

Lembar

🅰A5 🚌⛴From Padang Bai & Benoa Harbour ℹIn ferry terminal

Lombok's main sea port, in a bay surrounded by hills, is the gateway to the island for passenger car-ferries from Bali. Crowds of merchants and other travellers mill around Lembar's ferry terminus. Much lively haggling takes place over prices of seats in over-loaded buses and vans travelling to other destinations on Lombok. There is a small tourist office, some phones and a few food stalls. At the docks, beautiful Bugis schooners and small steamers load and unload cargo.

The roads around Lembar run through lush, rural scenery. The coast road, skirting the peninsula towards Sekotong some 10 km (6 miles) to the south, has good views of the bay and its *bagan*, stationary fishing platforms standing in the sea. Fishermen lower huge nets into which they attract fish with the aid of lanterns. From here skiffs take passengers to the remote coral islands of Gili Gede and Gili Nanggu.

Sweta

🅰B5 🚌 ℹMataram; (0370) 632 723 or 634 800

One of Lombok's oldest temples, Pura Lingsar, is in Sweta. First built in 1714, the large complex has both Balinese Hindu and Sasak Wetu Telu (Muslim) shrines, as well as a pond containing sacred albino eels. At the Bertais Market, fruits, vegetables and spices are displayed in all their colours. You can also bargain for baskets, textiles, bamboo products and more.

Narmada

🅰B5 🚌 ℹMataram; (0370) 632 723 or 634 800 🕐Daily

Built in 1805, Narmada was originally a raja's (king's) summer palace. In the

↑ The Miru Temple, set within the grounds of Narmada

gardens is a temple and a lake said to represent the crater lake of Gunung Rinjani. The lotus-filled ponds and terraced gardens recall royal splendours of the past.

Senggigi

🅰A5 🚌From Lembar & Mataram ℹMataram; (0370) 632 723 or 634 800

Senggigi was once the most popular resort in Lombok, but most tourists now prefer to head for the Gili Islands. Although very much less developed than Kuta in Bali, Senggigi has a broad range of accommodation, restaurants and entertainment facilities. Although Senggigi Beach is,

Sun setting over Batu Bolong Beach and the small temple just south of Senggigi ↑

strictly speaking, two glistening bays, separated by a thrust of white coral jutting out into the ocean, the area officially known as Senggigi is a 6-km (4-mile) strip of road and beachfront. Restaurants and cafés line the colourful main beach road.

The views up and down the coast, and out across the sea to Bali, which can be enjoyed from the coastal road, are majestic. Swimming off the beach is safe; and waves suitable for less experienced wave-riders peel to the left and right off the reef. Many people also windsurf here. Around the reef itself is a variety of marine life and beautiful coral. This is a good spot for relaxed snorkelling.

An atmospheric temple shrine stands on a black outcrop of rock reaching out

> **Tanjung is surrounded by lush countryside in which coconut groves alternate with picturesque rice fields and vegetable gardens.**

into the sea at Batu Bolong Beach, 3 km (2 miles) south of central Senggigi. The crimson sunsets are beautiful.

---

8 🖼️ 🛍️

Tanjung

🅰️ B4 🚌 From Mataram
ℹ️ Mataram; (0370) 632 723 or 634 800

Tanjung's livelihood is based on fishing as well as agricultural products. It is a large village on the road north to the Gunung Rinjani foothills, with a twice-weekly cattle market. Tanjung is surrounded by lush countryside in which coconut groves alternate with picturesque ricefields and vegetable gardens. In the river shallows grows *kangkung* (a leafy vegetable rather like watercress), one of Lombok's most popular dishes.

The road north from Tanjung runs along the black-sand beach and the terrain becomes distinctly arid. Some 4 km (2 miles) away on the coast is Krakas, famous for fresh, cool spring water. The spring is located underwater 400 m (1,320 ft) offshore at a

depth of about 10 m (33 ft). Further north, just past the small town of Gondang, are the Tiu Pupas waterfall and seven caves.

9

Segenter

🅰️ B4 🚌 From Mataram
ℹ️ Mataram; (0370) 632 723 or 634 800 🕘 9am–5pm daily

The small village of Segenter is a typical, traditional Lombok community, a good place to wander and see people going about their daily lives. The inhabitants maintain their old culture and traditions and are less commercially minded than those around Senggigi.

In the late morning, many villagers rest in the "guest huts", open structures with platforms above ground level, set between rows of the larger thatched houses which make up the village as a whole.

The people of Segenter produce most of the staple food necessary for their daily needs and plant cotton, rice and tobacco to sell at the market.

10 🍴

Sembalun

C4 From Mataram & Tanjung Mataram; (0370) 632 723 or 634 800

Lying in a valley surrounded by mountains is Sembalun, a village consisting of single-storey wooden buildings. Visitors are few, and there are only a couple of basic places to stay. There is a pleasant sense of remoteness. The air is fresh, and can be quite cold at night. This is a good place for walks. Shallots are grown here, and a pungent, but not unpleasant, scent pervades the valley.

From here the view of Gunung Rinjani is very vivid: the mountain seems to be almost within an arm's reach. Sembalun is the starting point of a Rinjani climb route more direct than that from Senaru, but the facilities here are not as good.

The road south to Sapit runs across one of the highest mountain passes in Indonesia. The hairpins and gradients give good views over the Sembalun Valley.

11

Bayan Beleq Mosque

C4 Beleq, Karang Bajo, Bayan

The oldest mosque on Lombok, this enchanting building near Beleq village was founded by Syeh Gaus Abdul Razak in 1634. It is comprised of a black sugar-palm fibre roof, decorated with a wooden crown, and woven bamboo walls resting upon a low stone wall. The natural materials have to be renewed every six years. The *meru*-shaped roof typifies the Javanese/Hindu influence that preceded Islam. Beside the mosque are the graves of some of the early followers of Wetu Telu, the syncretic Sasak form of Islam. The mosque is only used for religious ceremonies three times per year; at other times, visitors who wish to enter must speak to the caretaker.

12 🍴

Sapit

C4 From Sweta Mataram; (0370) 632 723 or 634 800

Sapit is situated on the eastern slopes of Gunung Rinjani at about 800 m (2,640 ft) above sea level. It is a refreshingly cool mountain resort commanding views of eastern Lombok, and of Sumbawa across the sea beyond. Blanketing Rinjani's lower slopes around Sapit are emerald-green rice terraces and tobacco plantations.

The village is basic, but gardens and flowerbeds make a fresh, orderly impression. There are some good, inexpensive guesthouses here.

13 🍴 💬 🛍

Senaru

C4 From Sweta & Tanjung Mataram; (0370) 632 723 or 634 800

At a height of over 400 m (1,320 ft) on the lower slopes of Gunung Rinjani, Senaru is braced by cool, refreshing air. From here the visitor is rewarded with perfect views of Rinjani to the south and the ocean to the west.

Once a secluded mountain settlement sheltered from the outside world, this village, with its traditional-style houses, has become a weekend escape from the heat of the coastal regions. With its many simple guesthouses and restaurants, it is the most popular departure point

→

The breathtaking Tiu Kelep waterfall on the outskirts of Senaru

for treks and climbs up the mountain. It is also possible to make arrangments for a trek through the Gunung Rinjani national park and up the volcano. Camping equipment, tent and sleeping-bag rental are available, porters and guides can be engaged and food and other necessities can be bought here.

An easy 30-minute walk to the west of Senaru leads to the dramatic 40 m- (132 ft-) high Sendanggile Waterfalls, where water comes straight off one of the highest peaks in Southeast Asia. Here is the chance to wade in what must be the cleanest and freshest water in Indonesia. A little further uphill is the Tiu Kelep waterfall, with a lovely pool perfect for swimming.

Another short 30-minute walk from the village centre is Payan, which has thatched huts and a megalithic appearance: this is one of Lombok's few remaining Wetu Telu villages. Although somewhat commercialized, it is an example of Lombok's aboriginal village traditions. Wetu Telu is a form of Islam

←

Hikers climbing Gunung Rinjani in the national park at Sembalun

mixing Islamic beliefs with pre-Islamic indigenous and Hindu-Buddhist elements. The Muslim practices observed at Payan contain both Balinese and Hindu elements. The women wear traditional sarongs and black shirts for weaving and during Muslim ceremonies.

---

14 🍴

Labuhan Lombok

🅰 C5 🚌 From Mataram 🚢 From Mataram and Sumbawa ℹ In ferry terminal

The bay around Labuhan Lombok forms a natural harbour. There are good views of Gunung Rinjani from here. A road runs parallel with the shore, and between it and the waterside are the settlements of Bugis fishermen consisting of houses on stilts. Colourfully painted trawlers are moored nearby. The forebears of this community came from South Sulawesi. The town's Sunday market sells all manner of produce and daily needs. At

one end of the bay, 2 km (1 mile) from the town, is the ferry jetty for services running east of Lombok to Sumbawa, the next island in the Lesser Sundas group.

EAT

Rinjani Lodge Restaurant
Guests enjoy spellbinding mountain views from tables and chairs or comfortable beanbags at this rustic eatery. Both local and international dishes are on the menu. Favourites include *gado-gado*, creamy pasta, cashew-nut chicken and chocolate lava cake.

🅰 C4 🏠 Jalan Pariwisata, Senaru 🌐 rinjanilodge.com/restaurant

Rp Rp Rp

15

Pringgasela

🅰C5 🚌From Sweta & Labuhan Lombok
ℹ️Mataram; (0370) 632 723 or 634 800

The shady Pringgasela village lies in the cool, quiet foothills of Gunung Rinjani. Many villagers here are weavers, happy for visitors to watch. Outside many of the houses colourful textiles are displayed for sale. The patterns and hues, predominantly blacks and reds, are characteristic of Lombok.

In the hills south of Pringgasela is another craft centre, Loyok, Lombok's premier basketware, bamboo and palm-leaf handicraft village. The road from Loyok runs parallel to a fast-flowing stream that runs through beautiful forests and valleys.

16

Tetebatu

🅰C5 🚌From Mataram
ℹ️Mataram; (0370) 632 723 or 634 800

A hill-station village, Tetebatu offers good views of Gunung Rinjani and has a relaxing

ambience. The village itself is quite modest, but over an area running 3–4 km (2–3 miles) up the mountain slope there are a number of guesthouses, set among rice fields.

Pleasant walks are to be had in the mountain air, passing large-leaved tobacco plantations. One hike runs to a small river into which flows the Jeruk Manis Waterfall – the route is quite strenuous but can be tackled by fit children over ten, as well as adults. Other walks lead to isolated villages and a tropical forest inhabited by monkeys. It is advisable to engage one of the guides who offer their services in the village.

17

Rembitan and Sade

🅰B6 ℹ️Mataram; (0370) 632 723 or 634 800

The farming villages of Rembitan and Sade, which are approximately 3 km (2 miles)

apart from one another, are both attractively set against the hillside. Despite the fact that many visitors stop here, and therefore sellers of souvenirs abound, Rembitan and Sade remain good places to catch a glimpse of traditional Sasak life, in which weaving textiles, growing rice and rearing goats and cattle are major occupations. A distinctive feature of the area is the *lumbung*, a bonnet-shaped rice barn. Once a symbol of Lombok, these barns are now less commonly seen. The walls of the thatch-roofed barns and houses are made of bamboo or palm-leaf ribs.

18 🍴 🍽️

Gerupuk

🅰B6 ℹ️Mataram; (0370) 632 723 or 634 800

The village of Gerupuk is situated on the edge of a long bay. Villagers mostly live in

> **Gerupuk is home to one of south Lombok's most popular surf breaks. In the bay, swells from the Indian Ocean build up and break on coral reefs, creating fine waves.**

TEXTILES IN LOMBOK

Hand-woven textiles, of very high quality, are produced in Lombok using traditional backstrap looms. The villages that specialize in textile-weaving are Sukarara, Pringgasela, Rembitan and Sade. There is some larger-scale production around Mataram. In the villages, the entire process of cloth-making can be watched by visitors, from the boiling of barks and roots to make dyes, and the soaking of cotton threads, to the weaving of original patterns on the hand-operated loom. The villagers use only natural plants for the dyes. Yellow dye, for example, is made from an extract of turmeric root, while blue comes from the indigo plant. Roots and bark are pounded and boiled; the cotton threads are immersed for 24 hours, and, when dry, are arranged on the loom in the manner demanded by the pattern of the textile.

simple reed huts and there is a mosque at the centre of the village. Gerupuk's main income, apart from fishing, comes from seaweed cultivation. The seaweed, which is used as an ingredient in food products for farm animals, grows on semi-submerged bamboo frames that are situated in the waters off the beach. After being harvested it can be seen drying in neat bundles along the roadside.

Gerupuk is home to one of south Lombok's most popular surf breaks. In the bay, swells from the Indian Ocean build up and break on coral reefs, creating fine waves. Surfers hire a small skiff for the short trip to the break, and the journey itself gives breath-

taking views of the nearby cliffs and rocky crags. The skiffs anchor a short distance from the break and await the surfers' return. The waves here are considered more user-friendly and forgiving than many of the others on this coast, where the sea can often be rough. They break on coral deep enough not to cause undue worry to board riders, unlike the shallow breaks and steep take-off points of Maui near Selong Blanak to the west. While the waves mostly break right, left breaks also peel off, although less regularly. The surf is at its best early in the morning before any wind gets up – usually before 9am – but even later in the day when cross-winds blow offshore, the waves are fine. The surfers who come here are mostly Japanese, Australians and locals from Kuta village; there is also a smattering of Brazilians and French.

←
A sea of green rice fields and coconut trees in the village of Tetebatu

19
Sukarara

A B5 **From Sweta**
i Mataram; (0370) 632 723 or 634 800

Many people in Sukarara earn their living by weaving *songket* textiles *(p136)*. Large numbers of shops display and sell many varieties of local cloth. Village women dressed in black will demonstrate their expertise with the loom and are willing to pose for photographs.

20
Penujak

A B5 **From Sweta**
i Mataram; (0370) 632 723 or 634 800

Along with Banyumulek *(p189)* and Masbagik, Penujak is one of Lombok's main pottery-producing villages, and perhaps the best place to see the process, which the villagers will explain. Traditionally, women made the pots by hand while the men marketed them. Now that export sales have led to increased output, men join in the production process. Each village produces its own distinct pottery, but all the designs are available in all three places.

↑ A villager creating a traditional pot in Penujak

EAT

Horizon at Ashtari

A Lombok landmark on a hilltop, Horizon Ashtari offers views of forest-clad hills. It serves Mediterranean dishes along with some local fare.

🅰B6 🏠Jalan Mawun Prabu, Kuta 🅦ashtarilombok.com

Ⓡ Ⓡ Ⓡ

Nugget's Corner

Serving Indonesian and Arab cuisine, Nugget's Corner is known for the bold flavours and beautiful presentation of its excellent dishes. It offers vegan options.

🅰B6 🏠Jalan Raya Kuta, Kuta 📞(0878) 9131 7431

Ⓡ Ⓡ Ⓡ

Warung Flora

This friendly, family-run eatery in an open-sided bamboo hut specializes in superb freshly caught fish. There are other local dishes on the menu too.

🅰B6 🏠Jalan Pariwisata Pantai Kuta, Kuta 📞(0878) 6350 0009

Ⓡ Ⓡ Ⓡ

Bucu Restaurant and Bar

In a bamboo building with a grass roof, this charming eatery serves Indonesian cuisine and succulent barbecue fare. Be sure to try the seafood curry or the barbecued steaks.

🅰B6 🏠Jalan Pariwisata Pantai Kuta, Kuta 📞(0878) 6591 4042

Ⓡ Ⓡ Ⓡ

㉑ 🍴 🖥 🛍

Kuta

🅰B6 🚌From Sweta
ℹ Mataram; (0370) 632 723 or 634 800

Lombok's Kuta was originally most famous for its surf, for it is here that the island's mellow waters meet the powerful currents of the Indian Ocean, forming world-class surf breaks.

When Lombok's international airport opened at Praya in 2011, Kuta became an easily accessible destination. It now has a wide choice of accommodation and restaurants alongside its picture-postcard white-sand beach, making it an ideal base for exploring the cliffs, headlands and beaches of the rugged southern coastline, set against a backdrop of hills spotted with tobacco fields.

The 7-km- (4-mile-) long bay extends to the white sandy beach of Putri Nyale, which rests spectacularly beside a craggy limestone pinnacle on the shores of a crystal-blue lagoon. The beach is famous for the ancient Sasak legend of Princess Mandalika. The beautiful princess is said to have been strongly desired by six of the rival princes of Lombok, and each had threatened to attack her father's kingdom if their proposals of marriage were rejected. On a moonlit night, in allegiance to her father and for the wellbeing of her people, the princess publicly flung herself into the ocean from the hilltop on the east side of the beach, sacrificing herself so that no prince could have her. Once her body touched the water, it was transformed into many colourful sea worms – celebrated during the annual Bau Nyale Festival held here.

㉒ 🖥

Tanjung Aan Beach

🅰B6 🏠8 km (5 miles) east of Kuta

The almost impossibly beautiful, white-powder-sand beach of Tanjung Aan is famous for its surf breaks. When the tide is out, the bay turns into shallow pools of turquoise water. Tanjung Aan

↑ The beautiful Tanjung Aan Beach, in southern Lombok, bathed in sunlight

↑ A local fisherman untangling his net on Mawun Beach

BAU NYALE FESTIVAL

Every February or March, when the forces of the sea and moon coincide, masses of *nyale* – luminous sea worms – arrive and reproduce in the moonlight off Putri Nyale Beach. The rare *nyale* is considered a great delicacy. Hundreds of Sasak people assemble on the beach for an all-night feast, during which the worms are eaten grilled, fried or sometimes even raw.

encompasses two bays: Aan to the west and Pedau to the east, separated by a rocky outcrop. The waters offer safe opportunities for swimming and snorkelling, but there can be a strong current on the eastern bay. Cafés on the pristine beach offer tables and sunbeds.

Check out Bukit Meresek, a hill at the western end of the bay with a lovely view at sunset, as well as Batu Payung – an extraordinary, towering, coastal landform on the eastern point with large, striking rock formations.

23 🖂

Mawun Beach

🅐 B6 🚗 10 km (6 miles) west of Kuta

Though the approach to Mawun is down a long, pot-holed road, the serenity of the secluded beach is well worth it. Mawun is one of the most picturesque beaches in south Lombok. Here, a horseshoe-shaped crescent of white sand borders a perfect half-moon bay, sheltered by two massive headlands, all of which make the generally calm turquoise waters popular for swimming. However, when the swell is large enough, there are good right-hand and left-hand barrels for surfing. There are some large shade trees and small *warung* here serving simple local dishes; they also rent out sunbeds and umbrellas.

㉔ Bangko Bangko

🅰️A5 🚌From Lembar
ℹ️Mataram; (0370) 632 723
or 634 800

A popular place for fishing and surfing, Bangko Bangko lies at the end of a peninsula at the southwest extremity of Lombok. It can be reached only along a dirt road. The reward for this trip somewhat off the beaten track is the spectacular scenery.

Some surfers have named the area Desert Point. The waves that peel to the left off a coral shelf, before slamming into the base of the cliff face, provide great conditions for experienced riders. The unpredictable, often dangerous seas are good for game fishing. A fishing trip can be booked via tour operators in Lembar.

㉕ Selong Blanak

🅰️B6 ℹ️Mataram; (0370) 632 723 or 634 800

Marked at each end by rocky promontories, Selong Blanak is a tranquil bay with a fishing settlement and tourist accommodation and facilities.

PICTURE PERFECT
Coastal Views

Sempiak Hill, which rises above the beach at Selong Blanak, offers a great vantage point from which to take photos of the breath-taking coastline.

On the beach are multi-coloured outrigger canoes. Most people come here to surf at the nearby Maui beach. The waves are exceptionally fast. Because of the steep take-offs and the fact that the waves are ridden over very shallow coral, this is a place for very experienced surfers only.

㉖ 🍴 🍵 🏠 Tanjung Luar

🅰️C5 ℹ️Mataram; (0370) 632 723 or 634 800

The village of Tanjung Luar earns its living from the sea. It is a minor port – travellers from nearby islands land here by means of an inter-island taxi service which uses small outriggers. Many occupations to do with fishing and the sea are represented here and there is a busy fish market. Fishermen return to port after spending several days afloat, and sell their catch beside the water's edge. It is possible to watch huge sharks being brought to shore. Contributing to the lively atmosphere are the salt-sellers, the children fishing off the main jetty, and the people giving their boats a new coat of paint.

A short walk from the fish market, lining the beachfront, live some Bugis communities, their wooden houses raised on stilts. Colourful Bugis schooners, with distinctive high prows, lie at anchor here.

For many people in Tanjung Luar, *cidomo* are the only form of transport. These are small horse-drawn buggies, brightly painted and often decorated with vivid red pompoms and tassels.

> **Still relatively undeveloped, the southwestern Gili Islands offer a natural environment of idyllic beaches and abundant corals.**

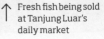
↑ Fresh fish being sold at Tanjung Luar's daily market

Sun setting over a fishing boat moored off the island of Gili Asahan ↑

27 (🖐)

Banyumulek

🅰 B5 🚌 From Mataram
ℹ Mataram; (0370) 632 723 or 634 800

This village of wooden huts with thatched roofs is a centre for the production of hand-made terracotta pots. Here, visitors can see how they are made and roam among the displays of pots, some decorated with textiles and rattan. Buyers of items too large to carry can have them shipped abroad if necessary.

About 3 km (2 miles) west of Banyumulek, an easy climb up Gunung Pengsong leads to a good view. From the Hindu shrine at the top, Bali's Gunung Agung and Lombok's Gunung Rinjani are visible in opposite directions. On one side the plain of Mataram stretches to the sea; on the other is an arc of rugged mountains.

---

28 (🍴)(🍹)

Southwestern Gili Islands

🅰 A5 🚤 from Tembowong, Senggigi or Lembar

Sprinkled off the north shore of Lombok's southwestern tip are the "Secret Gilis", two groups of tiny emerald islands. Gili Nanggu, Gili Genting and Gili Tangkong form part of the cluster close to Lembar, while Gili Gede, Gili Asahan and Gili Poh constitute a little archipelago further west, just off the coast near Pelangan.

While some of the islands are sparsely inhabited, others are not much more than rocky prominences. All have white-sand beaches, peppered with palm trees, cowrie shells and ghost crabs. Still relatively untouched, they offer a natural environment of idyllic beaches and abundant corals.

Gili Gede (*gede* means "big") is the largest and best-known island off the Sekotong Peninsula, and it also has the widest selection of accommodation options, comprising a number of cottage-style hotels and homestays. There are no motorized vehicles. This is a working island; the villages are actively involved in pearl farming and fishing.

Gili Nanggu is very quiet, and perfect for diving, snorkelling or just relaxing, with just a few simple cottages on the beach and a restaurant. On Gili Asahan there is an eco-resort, several beach-bungalow hotels, a couple of restaurants and some excellent dive spots, such as Secret Garden, Sanking Point and Belongan, with its cluster of coral pinnacles.

A daily fastboat runs from Bali to Gili Gede and there are boat services from Tembowong Harbour, Senggigi and Lembar in Lombok to the other Southwestern Gili islands.

> 💬 INSIDER TIP
> **Selong Blanak Buffaloes**
>
> Visitors to Selong Blanak Beach can often witness the magnificent sight of a large herd of water buffaloes being ushered along the sand from one grazing ground to another by a team of Sasak cowboys late in the afternoon.

NEED TO KNOW

Food vendor stalls in the rain, Kuta, Bali

BEFORE
YOU GO

Forward planning is essential to any successful trip. Be prepared for all eventualities by considering the following points before you travel.

AT A GLANCE

CURRENCY
Indonesian
Rupiah (IDR)

AVERAGE DAILY SPEND

SAVE	SPEND	SPLURGE
Rp590,000/ US$40	Rp1170,000/ US$80	Rp3650,000/ US$250

BOTTLED WATER Rp10,000/ US$0.66	COFFEE Rp30,000/ US$2	BEER Rp30,000/ US$2	DINNER FOR TWO Rp700,000/ US$46

ESSENTIAL PHRASES

Good morning	Selamat pagi
Goodbye	Selamat tinggal
Excuse me	Permisi
Thank you	Terima kasih
I don't understand	Saya tidak mengerti
Please	Silahkan

ELECTRICITY SUPPLY

Voltage is 220 Volts, 50Hz. Plugs and sockets are the European two-pronged variety.

Passports and Visas

The citiziens of 140 countries (including the USA, the UK, Australia and New Zealand) do not need a visa to enter Indonesia and are allowed free entry for up to 30 days. This cannot be extended once you are there. For stays longer than 30 days you need to apply for a visa at your nearest Indonesian consulate or embassy before you travel. For the latest regulations and to check whether you are eligible for a free visa of up to 30 days, visit **Bali.com**. It is essential that your passport is valid for a minimum of six months after your intended date of departure from Indonesia.
Bali.com
🔳 bali.com/visa-indonesia-entry-requirements-bali.html

Travel Safety Advice

Visitors can get up-to-date travel safety information from the UK Foreign and Commonwealth Office, the US State Department and the Australian Department of Foreign Affairs and Trade.
AUS
🔳 smartraveller.gov.au
UK
🔳 gov.uk/foreign-travel-advice
US
🔳 travel.state.gov

Customs Information

There are restrictions on the import and export of products such as ivory, crocodile skin and turtle shell, on items made from endangered species and on the export of antiquities and certain cultural objects. An invidual is permitted to carry the following within Indonesia for personal use:
Tobacco products 200 cigarettes (or 50 cigars or 100 grams of tobacco)
Alcohol 1 litre
Cash Cash in any currency equivalent to Rp100 million (US$6,800) or more must be declared on entry or exit

Insurance

It is essential to take out insurance covering medical issues, and wise to have coverage for theft, loss of belongings, cancellation and delays. Check that coverage includes medical evacuation: treatment of serious conditions often requires an emergency transfer to Singapore.

Vaccinations

The only vaccine required by international regulations is yellow fever. Proof of vaccination is only required if you have visited a country in the yellow-fever zone (some parts of Africa and South America) within six days prior to entering Indonesia. Cholera, hepatitis A, typhoid and polio inoculations are recommended, and tetanus shots should be up to date. Dengue fever has been reported in Bali and Lombok, and malaria is a real risk in Lombok, so consult your doctor about preventive medication well before you begin your trip.

Money

Bali and Lombok use the Indonesian Rupiah (IDR) as their main currency. Credit cards are broadly accepted, and ATMs are widely available. Small shops, cafés and taxi drivers often expect the customer to provide exact change.

Booking Accommodation

Online booking is available for nearly all accommodation in Bali and Lombok. For more remote accommodation – on the offshore islands – online booking is not always reliable, so it's worth double-checking by phone. During the peak seasons of July, August and Christmas, accommodation costs rise and booking well in advance is advisable.

Travellers with Specific Needs

Provisions for disabled people are, as in much of Asia, inadequate. Wheelchair access is very rare. Pavements are high and uneven. Many public places are accessed by steps; very few have ramps, and wheelchair users will find public transport inaccessible. The more up-market hotels and villas, however, are slowly becoming increasingly aware of the needs of disabled travellers. The following tour operator makes specialist arrangements:

Bali Access Travel
w baliaccesstravel.com
Accessible Indonesia
w accessibleindonesia.org

Language

The most widely spoken languages in Bali are Indonesian and Balinese, and in Lombok, Indonesian and Sasak. English is the main foreign language spoken.

Closures

Government offices in Bali Open 8am–3pm Mon–Thu, 8am–noon Fri, closed Sat and Sun.

Business and government offices in Lombok Open 9am–4pm Mon–Fri. As it is a Muslim island, most offices will close between 11.30am and 2pm on Friday for prayers at the mosque.

Banking hours Open 9am–3pm Mon–Fri, some banks open until noon Sat.

Public holidays All banks and government offices close on public holidays but most shops and private businesses operate as normal.

Shops Open from morning till evening daily.

PUBLIC HOLIDAYS	
1 Jan	New Year's Day
7 Mar	Bali Hindu New Year
3 Apr	Isra Mi'raj
1 May	Labour Day
19 May	Waisak Day
1 Jun	Pancasila Day
5 Jun	Hari Raya Idul Fitri
6 Jun	Lebaran Holiday
12 Aug	Idul Adha
17 Aug	Independence Day
30 Aug	Islamic New Year
10 Nov	Prophet Muhammad's Birthday
25 Dec	Christmas Day

GETTING AROUND

Whether you are making a flying visit, or heading off on a lengthy adventure, discover how best to reach your destination.

AT A GLANCE

PUBLIC TRANSPORT COSTS

KUTA TO UBUD

Rp250,000

Metered taxi fare

KUTA TO UBUD

Rp60,000

Shuttle Bus

KUTA TO UBUD

Rp300,000

Car and Driver

Note: Journey times can vary considerably according to traffic

SPEED LIMIT

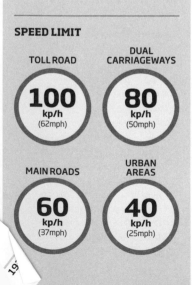

TOLL ROAD

100 kp/h (62mph)

DUAL CARRIAGEWAYS

80 kp/h (50mph)

MAIN ROADS

60 kp/h (37mph)

URBAN AREAS

40 kp/h (25mph)

Arriving by Air

Flying to Bali

Bali's only airport is **Ngurah Rai International Airport**, situated 13 km (8 miles) south of Denpasar. It is also often referred to as Denpasar International Airport. Major international airlines serving Bali's airport include Garuda Indonesia (Indonesia's national carrier), Air Asia, Air New Zealand (seasonal), American Airlines, ANA, Cathay Pacific Airways, China Airlines, China Southern, Delta, Emirates, Eva Air, Jetstar, KLM, Korean Air, Lion Air, Malaysia Airlines, Philippine Airlines, Qatar Airways, Royal Brunei, Singapore Airlines, Thai Airways International, Virgin Australia and Xiamen Airlines. There are frequent direct flights from Australia and some countries in East Asia, such as Singapore, Thailand and Japan. Other carriers go no further than Jakarta, but they may make onward connections to Denpasar via Garuda Indonesia. There are many daily flights between Jakarta and Denpasar. Many travellers from Europe fly to Singapore, from where there are direct flights every day to Denpasar on Garuda Indonesia and Singapore Airlines. Carriers from Taiwan (China Airlines) and Hong Kong (Cathay Pacific Airways) stop in their own capital cities.

Ngurah Rai International Airport
W bali-airport.com

Flying to Lombok

Lombok's Zainuddin Abdul Madjid Airport, near Mataram, is mainly served by domestic flights from other parts of Indonesia. The easiest and fastest way to get from Bali to Lombok (and vice versa from Lombok to Bali) is via a quick flight. Flight times from Bali's Ngurah Rai International Airport to Lombok take only around 25 minutes. SilkAir flies directly between Lombok and Singapore and Air Asia flies directly between Lombok and Kuala Lumpur. Garuda Indonesia has an international network of flights that serve Jakarta and Surabaya, from where you must connect to a domestic flight to Lombok.

Zainuddin Abdul Madjid Airport
W lombok-airport.co.id

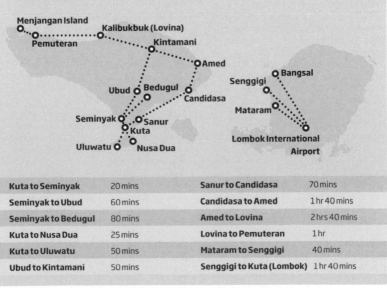

GETTING TO AND FROM THE AIRPORT

Airport	Destination	Taxi Fare	Journey Time
Bali Airport	Kuta	Rp120,000	15 mins
	Seminyak	Rp150,000	25 mins
	Sanur	Rp175,000	25 mins
	Canggu	Rp300,000	40 mins
	Ubud	Rp350,000	60 mins
	Candidasa	Rp450,000	1 hr 40 mins
	Lovina	Rp600,000	1 hr 50 mins
	Amed	Rp 800,000	2 hrs 50 mins
Lombok Airport	Senggigi	Rp220,000	1 hr 20 mins
	Mataram	Rp160,000	50 mins
	Kuta	Rp90,000	30 mins
	Bangsal Harbour	Rp350,000	1 hr 30 mins

ROAD JOURNEY PLANNER

Plotting the main driving routes according to journey time, this map is a handy reference for travelling between Bali and Lombok's main destinations by car. The times given reflect the fastest and most direct routes available.

Kuta to Seminyak	20 mins	Sanur to Candidasa	70 mins
Seminyak to Ubud	60 mins	Candidasa to Amed	1 hr 40 mins
Seminyak to Bedugul	80 mins	Amed to Lovina	2 hrs 40 mins
Kuta to Nusa Dua	25 mins	Lovina to Pemuteran	1 hr
Kuta to Uluwatu	50 mins	Mataram to Senggigi	40 mins
Ubud to Kintamani	50 mins	Senggigi to Kuta (Lombok)	1 hr 40 mins

195

Local Transport

Public transport in Bali and Lombok is cheap, but not always convenient for visitors, since it becomes scarce after dark, and the routes are designed to serve the needs of the local population rather than tourists.

Buses

Buses, used mainly by locals, operate long-distance inter-city and inter-island routes. The main routes are from Denpasar to Singaraja, Denpasar to Amlapura and Sweta to Labuhan Lombok. Fares (non-negotiable) are paid to the driver or the conductor. Tickets cannot be bought in advance except for inter-island trips. The main terminals in South Bali are around Denpasar: at Batubulan in north Denpasar; at Kereneng in central Denpasar; and at Ubung in west Denpasar.

Bemos

Bemos are minivans that drive along pre-determined routes. Small *bemos* service a town while large *bemos* travel between towns, such as from Denpasar to Ubud or Kuta. Fares are low (less than Rp10,000 within a town and less than Rp20,000 between towns), but it may take several hours to cover a distance of 15 km (10 miles) and tourists are sometimes overcharged. *Bemos* are often very hot and crowded, and do not tend to adhere to set routes and times. They are generally not favoured by tourists or those on a tight itinerary.

Tourist Shuttles

Tourist shuttles – minivans or minibuses that travel between tourist destinations at regular intervals – are a very convenient way to get around Bali and Lombok. They are also a good way to meet other travellers. A tourist bus typically seats between eight and twenty people. Several companies, such as **Perama**, run services between the major tourist destinations on a regular schedule at reasonable prices (fares range from Rp35,000 to Rp175,000). **Kura-Kura Bus** (fares from Rp20,000) is a Japanese-owned tourist shuttle bus service connecting the popular tourist areas of Kuta, Legian, Seminyak, Sanur, Ubud, Jimbaran and Nusa Dua. It is preferable to book in advance.

These tourist shuttle bus services, combined with public ferries, run between the main tourist destinations on Lombok, such as Senggigi and Kuta, and those in South Bali and the Gili Islands.

Perama
🔲 peramatour.com/transport/shuttle
Kura-Kura Bus
🔲 kura2bus.com

Boats and Ferries

Although the islands of Bali and Lombok seem quite near to each other, the ocean between them can get very rough. Boat and ferry operators change constantly and it is a good idea to do some research on the ground for the ones that adhere to best safety practices.

The cheapest way to cross the Lombok Straits is by ferry, although the voyage takes the best part of a day. Ferries travel from Padang Bai in East Bali to Pelabuhan Lembar (Lembar Harbour) in Lombok at 60- to 90-minute intervals. The crossing takes four hours (or longer, depending on conditions). It is worth getting to Padang Bai well in advance in order to board one of the newer (and more reputable) ferries. Seating is available in an air-conditioned saloon; however, this is not as pleasant as being on the deck. Tickets are purchased at the harbour.

There are multiple fast boat companies travelling between Bali and Lombok; Bali and Gili Air, Gili Trawangan and Gili Meno; Bali and Gili Gede; Bali and Nusa Lembongan; and Bali and Nusa Penida. Departures are from Benoa, Serangan, Padang Bai and Amed. Fast boats to Nusa Lembongan and Nusa Penida depart from Sanur. Prices are competitive but choose one that has a good reputation and guarantees you a seat (as some companies overload their boats).

Cruises

Various companies operate cruises off Bali and Lombok. **Bali Hai** offers day cruises from Benoa Harbour to Lembongan, Nusa Penida and Nusa Ceningan islands. These include transport from and back to your hotel. They operate glass-bottomed catamarans for viewing coral reefs. Cruise options include watersports activities and dolphin-watching.
Bali Hai
🔲 balihaicruises.com

Taxis

In South Bali and in Senggigi on Lombok, metered taxis with air-conditioning can easily be flagged down in busy areas or ordered by phone or via an app. Taxis are much scarcer elsewhere, including major towns such as Ubud. Sometimes drivers will try to negotiate a flat fee, but it is usually cheaper to use the meter. Reliable companies are **Blue Bird Taxi** and **Grab** whose drivers also speak good English. It's best to avoid taxis where the driver refuses to use a meter.
Blue Bird Taxi
🔲 bluebirdgroup.com/my-blue-bird/
Grab
🔲 grab.com/id

Private Transport in Bali and Lombok

Having your own transport opens up a range of exciting possibilities for travel in Bali and Lombok, not least the chance for unscheduled detours, spur-of-the-moment stops and forays off the beaten track. Traffic conditions are daunting for the uninitiated, however, so renting a car with a local driver (which can be done for around Rp900,000/US$70 per day) is often the best option.

Driving

If you plan on driving in Indonesia you must have an International Driving Permit, which is best obtained in your own country if you already have a valid driver's licence. If you plan to drive a motorcycle, ensure that your International Driving Permit includes a motorcycle permit – this is better than going through the laborious process of obtaining a motorcycle permit in Bali. If you have an accident when driving without a valid international licence, you will not be covered by your travel insurance policy.

Car Rental

Self-drive cars are available in the main tourist areas where rental companies and tourist agencies rent cars at reasonable prices. You won't be allowed to take a rented car from Bali to Lombok or vice versa. The car rental company will deliver the car to you and pick it up at the end of the rental period. Always test-drive the car and check that it is in good working order before paying.

Parking

Parking in towns and at markets is supervised by a parking attendant who collects a small fee (generally Rp2,000–10,000 depending on the vehicle) and helps you get back onto the road.

Motorbikes

Motorbikes are widely available for rent, and can be particularly good for getting around in more isolated areas, especially in Nusa Penida and South Lombok where the roads are rough and potholed. Traffic conditions can be hazardous, however, so inexperienced riders should think twice before renting a bike. An international driving permit valid for motorbikes is required.

Helmets must be worn by law but the cheap ones provided by rental agencies offer little protection, so bring your own or buy a good one from a local shop, especially one with a face shield for protection from sun, rain, bugs and dust. Drive slowly and very carefully, as more and more people are injured or killed every year in accidents.

If you do not want to drive a motorbike yourself, you can hire an *ojek* (motorbike taxi) – these are more common in Lombok than Bali. They are best on quiet country roads but may be a bit precarious in the large towns. *Ojeks* do not have a meter so you need to agree a set price before you start your journey. If the operator doesn't provide you with a helmet do not get on the bike. You can book an *ojek* via the **Go-Jek** app.
Go-Jek
🆆 go-jek.com

Rules of the Road

Indonesians drive on the left-hand side of the road. In the event of an accident, the foreigner will very likely be deemed liable even if he or she is not at fault. Traffic regulations and driving conventions do not always coincide in practice: motorbikes overtake on either side; drivers pull out into traffic without looking – they expect you to avoid them. Right of way belongs to whoever is bigger or flashes their lights first.

As the pavements (sidewalks) are scarce and narrow, pedestrian traffic flows onto the roads, and includes livestock, pushcarts, religious processions and cyclists going the wrong way. In Lombok, traffic is much lighter, but you must watch out for pony carts. It is normal practice to sound the horn briefly before overtaking. At intersections where you are going straight ahead rather than turning, hazard lights should be used. In towns, one-way systems are increasingly common.

Driving just after dark is generally inadvisable because of poor visibility and, in particular, the inadequate lighting on bicycles and motor-cycles. Drivers should watch out for piles of black sand on the road (dumped there for the next day's building activities).

Cycling

Extreme caution must be exercised on busy roads, where bicycles are at the very bottom of the traffic hierarchy, especially in Bali. In Lombok the traffic is generally less chaotic throughout the island. A bicycle is a very enjoyable way to explore quieter areas but care should be taken as potholes and other obstacles abound.

Plenty of bicycles are available for rent in all the tourist areas, but before you pay for one, make sure the wheels are properly aligned, the brakes work well and that there is a working light. Ask your hotel to recommend a bike rental firm. Wear a helmet for extra safety, and try not to ride at night because roads are very poorly lit, or not lit at all.

PRACTICAL
INFORMATION

A little local know-how goes a long way in Bali and Lombok. Here you will find all the essential advice and information you will need during your stay.

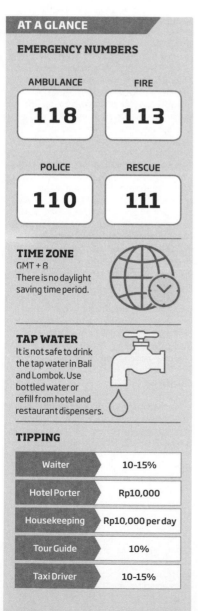

AT A GLANCE

EMERGENCY NUMBERS

AMBULANCE	FIRE
118	**113**

POLICE	RESCUE
110	**111**

TIME ZONE
GMT + 8
There is no daylight saving time period.

TAP WATER
It is not safe to drink the tap water in Bali and Lombok. Use bottled water or refill from hotel and restaurant dispensers.

TIPPING

Waiter	10–15%
Hotel Porter	Rp10,000
Housekeeping	Rp10,000 per day
Tour Guide	10%
Taxi Driver	10–15%

Personal Security

Tourists in Bali and Lombok are generally treated as valued guests, although caution should be exercised in South Lombok. Violent crime is rare, but bag-snatchings and pickpocketing can occur in tourist areas. Be very careful with your belongings, and beware of motorbike-mounted snatch thieves. Report any theft to the English-speaking tourist police if you wish to make an insurance claim. Avoid travelling alone late at night off the beaten track. Women travelling alone should exercise the usual precautions.

Health

Healthcare provision is generally poor in the remote areas, though there are good – if expensive – private clinics in Bali, including the International SOS Medical Centre. Pharmacies can often provide advice for minor ailments. Minor stomach upsets, caused by unfamiliar food and climate, and poor hygiene, are the commonest issue. Rest and rehydration are the main treatments; seek advice from a pharmacy or clinic if there is no improvement after a couple of days. Mosquitoes are a nuisance, so cover up in the evenings and use repellent.

Smoking, Alcohol and Drugs

Smoking is generally not allowed indoors in public places such as air-conditioned restaurants. Alcohol is widely available in tourist areas, and socially acceptable – though homebrew *arak* is sometimes dangerously tainted and should be avoided. It's not unusual for tourists to receive unsolicited offers of illegal drugs on the streets, especially in Kuta, Bali. Possession can result in lengthy prison sentences – or extortion by corrupt officials.

ID

Tourists are not legally required to carry ID, though it is advisable to carry at least a photocopy of some form of official identification, particularly when travelling outside of the main tourist areas.

Local Customs

The Balinese are an extrovert, cheerful people and will make visitors very welcome as long as they behave with due respect. The Sasaks of Lombok are more reserved and have strived hard to preserve their traditions and culture. As far as possible, do not express anger or behave in a confrontational manner as the Balinese find this very distasteful. Indonesians frown on public displays of private affection – these are considered embarrassing to others and therefore rude. Intimacy is kept behind doors, especially in Lombok. Holding hands is not customary for couples; however, linking arms is the norm.

Overly revealing clothing is frowned upon, so dress modestly. Avoid touching someone on the head – the head is considered sacred. Pass things with your right hand, rather than your left hand as the left hand is considered unclean. Do not point at someone (this is considered very rude) but beckon people by extending your hand and using a downward waving motion.

Visiting Sacred Sites

Hindus in Bali and Lombok observe strict rules in regard to their temples, which must be observed by everyone, including visitors, for safeguarding the spiritual hygiene of sacred places. These rules mainly concern dress requirements and conditions of *sebel* (taboo).

A waist sash and, in many places, a sarong, is the dress required of anyone entering a temple. These may be borrowed (or rented for a small charge) at temples that regularly accept tourists, but it is easy to buy your own almost anywhere. Conditions of *sebel* are: menstruation or having an open wound – this relates to a prohibition on shedding blood in a temple; bringing food into a temple as it clashes with offerings; and being physically or mentally ill.

LGBT

LGBT travellers are accepted throughout Bali. In particular in South Bali and Ubud there is a large LGBT expat community. Seminyak has a large number of gay nightclubs and other venues. Gay visitors should follow the same advice as all travellers and avoid public displays of affection.

In Lombok, which is mainly Muslim, homosexuality is largely frowned upon. The exception is the Gili Islands, where there is a more laid-back attitude.

Mobile Phones and Wi-Fi

Wi-Fi is now ubiquitous in the tourist areas, with nearly every hotel, restaurant, and café providing a free connection. International GSM mobile phones usually have coverage in Bali and Lombok. Pre-paid local SIM cards are also readily available from phone shops. It is necessary to show proof of ID to buy a local SIM card, and vendors will generally set it up for you if you have an unlocked phone.

Post

Post offices are available in all the tourist areas. Letters and postcards can take up to two weeks to reach destinations. It is possible to send parcels through post offices, but couriers such as DHL and UPS are faster and more reliable.

Taxes and Refunds

A 10% per cent sales tax is usually included in the marked price of retail goods, though some hotels and high-end restaurants add it to the bill at the end plus 11% service charge. No tax refunds are available for departing visitors.

WEBSITES AND APPS

bali.com
Check out the useful information on where to eat, sleep and play on this website.

lombok-tourism.com
An online guide to Lombok.

expat.or.id
This website provides plenty of practical information for expats planning to move to or already living in Indonesia.

balitourismboard.org
Bali's official tourism board website

INDEX

GLOSSARY

ARCHITECTURE

atap: palm-leaf thatched roof
bale: pavilion
candi bentar: split gate
gedong: enclosed pavilion
kori: roofed gate
kori agung: grand gate
kulkul: drum tower
meru: multitiered shrine
padmasana: tall shrine to the Supreme Deity
pelinggih: shrine, spirit house
pura: temple
puri: palace, house of nobility
rumah: house
wantilan: public pavilion with double roof
warung: coffee stall, small shop

ARTS AND CRAFTS

geringsing: warp- and weft-dyed textile, "double ikat"
ikat: warp resist-dyed textile
kayu: wood
lontar: type of palm; palm-leaf book
lukisan: painting
mas: gold
pande: metalsmith
paras: volcanic stone used for building and statuary
patung: statue
perak: silver
prada: gilt-painted cloth
songket: textile with supplementary weft thread, often gold or silver
tapel: mask
tenunan: weaving

MUSIC AND DANCE

arja: Balinese opera
baris: classical solo male dance
baris gede: a sacred dance for rows of male dancers
Barong: large sacred effigy danced by two men
belaganjur: processional percussion orchestra
gambuh: ancient court dance
gamelan: percussion orchestra
gangsa: bronze-keyed instrument
kebyar: vigorous style of gamelan music; vigorous solo dance
kendang: drum
keris: sacred wavy-bladed dagger
legong: classical dance for three females
prembon: mixed programme
Rangda: sacred demonic effigy, consort of the Barong
rejang: sacred dance for rows of female dancers
suling: bamboo flute
tari: dance

topeng: masked dance based on geneological tales
trompong: bronze instrument with 8 to 12 kettle gongs
wayang kulit: shadow puppet theatre
wayang wong: masked dance based on Hindu epics

DRESS

baju: shirt, dress
baju kaus: T-shirt
destar: head cloth for Balinese males
gelungan: ornate headdress
jilbab: head cloth for Muslim females
kain: cloth; long hip cloth, unsewn
kebaya: traditional jacket for females
peci: hat for Muslim males
sarong: sewn long hip cloth
selendang: ceremonial temple sash
sepatu: shoes

RELIGIONS AND COMMUNITY

banjar: village association
hari raya: any religious holiday
karya: work, especially collective ritual work
mesjid: mosque
odalan: temple festival
pedanda: high priest
pemangku: temple priest
penjor: festooned bamboo pole
pura dalem: temple of the netherworld
pura desa: village temple
pura puseh: temple of origins
sebel: taboo
sunat: Islamic ritual circumcision
tirta: holy water
yadnya: Hindu ritual (generic)

FOOD

air minum: drinking water
ayam: chicken
babi guling: roast pig
babi: pork
bakar: grilled
bebek tutu: smoked spicy duck
buah-buahan: fruit
cumi-cumi: squid
daging: meat
gado gado: vegetarian dish with peanut sauce
garam: salt
goreng: fried
gula: sugar
ikan laut: fish
jeruk nyepis: lime
jeruk: orange; citrus
kelapa: coconut
kopi: coffee
makan: eat
mie: noodles

minum: drink
nasi: food; rice; rice meal
pedas: hot (spicy)
pisang: banana
roti: bread
sambal: spicy condiment
sapi: beef
sate, sate lilit: small skewers of barbecued meat
susu: milk
teh: tea
telur: egg
udang: prawn, shrimp

NATURE AND LANDSCAPE

bukit: hill
burung: bird
danau: lake
gunung: mountain
hujan: rain
jalan: road
laut: sea
mata hari: sun
pantai: beach
pohon: tree
sawah: ricefield
subak: irrigation cooperative
sungai: river, stream
taman: garden, park
tanah: ground, earth, soil

TRAVEL AND TRANSPORT

bemo: public minibus
cidomo: rubber-tyred pony cart (in Lombok)
dokar: pony cart
jukung: outrigger sailing canoe
mobil: car
sepeda motor: motorcycle

MISCELLANEOUS

adat: customary law
bagus: good, handsome
baik: good
Bapak: polite term of address for a man
bayar: pay
cantik: pretty
dingin: cold
Ibu: polite term of address for a woman
mahal: expensive
murah: inexpensive
panas: hot, warm
pariwisata: tourism
puputan: suicidal fight-to-the-end
roko: cigarette
sakit: hurt; sick
selamat jalan: farewell ("on your journey")
terima kasih: thank you
tidak: no, not
tidur: sleep
uang: money

ACKNOWLEDGMENTS

The publisher would like to thank the following for their kind permission to reproduce their photographs:

Key: a-above; b-below/bottom; c-centre; f-far; l-left; r-right; t-top

123RF.com: balinature 88cl; Florian Blümm 152bl; iferol 159t; ivohausner 105tr; Ronnachai Limpakdeesavasd 11cr; Aleksandar Todorovic 66bl, 74tr, 82br.

4Corners: Jürgen Ritterbach 122–3b.

Alamy Stock Photo: 24BY36 36b; Konstantin Andreev 11t, 84–5b, 108tl; ART Collection 54t; Art Directors & TRIP 52cl, 52clb; Putu Artana 53tl; Arterra Picture Library 24cr, 121clb, 164b; Artokoloro Quint Lox Limited 55cra; Asia File 34–5t; AsiaDreamPhoto 231t; Aurora Photos 36tr; Romina Bayer 174br; Sabena Jane Blackbird 129tr; Paul Brown 22tl; pavlos christoforou 20cl; Chronicle 56br; Sue Clark 129br; Thomas Cockrem 42t, 55tl, 73br, 178bl; Cultura Creative (RF) 47b; Leila Cutler 132clb; David Buch Photography 39cl; Chris Deeney 41t; Design Pics Inc 45cl; Marius Dobilas 86tr; Brad Downs 27tl; Eagle Visions Photography / Craig Lovell 22–3t, 161t; Peter Eastland 20bl, 73tr, 132bl; Martyn Evans 37br; Dima Fadeev 28bl; Michele Falzone 50bl, 66–7, 108–9b; Christine Gates 150br; Sioen Gérard 127tr; GoSeeFoto 78br; Hagen Production 41cl; Vince Harris 165tr; Hemis 13br; Horizon Images / Motion 70–1t, 86–7b; KC Hunter 100–101; imageBROKER 139tr; INTERFOTO 55bl; Ivoha 43cr; Jango / Stockimo 103cla; JHMimaging 37tl; John Warburton-Lee Photography 106cl; Jon Arnold Images Ltd 137br, 185cla; Kenishirotie 38br; John Kershaw 45br; Ronnachai Limpakdeesavasd 121br; Christoph Lischetzki 30cl, 106bl; LOOK Die Bildagentur der Fotografen GmbH 26tr, 100cra, 184b; Edmund Lowe 20t, 110–11; MARKA 104tl; Stefano Politi Markovina 185br; master2 180bl; mauritius images GmbH 98bl; Annette Maya 153br; Aliaksandr Mazurkevich 24t, 40br; Military History Collection 56–7t, 57clb; Igor Mojzes 39crb; Denis Moskvinov 47cl, 52cr; Roberto Nistri 95br; Nokuro 143tr; Angela Nott 95cla; Agung Parameswara 130–31b; Carlos Peñalba 172–3; Photononstop 153crb; Peter Pinnock 149bc; Christian Platzer 26tl; Juergen Ritterbach 105b; robertharding 41br, 43cla, 49cla, 55cb, 140t, 158br; RooM the Agency 27tr, 172clb; Reynaldo Santa 150t; Norbert Scanella 156–7t; Peter Schickert 28cr; sculpies 53bl; Leonid Serebrennikov 43tr, 107t, 136–7t; Simon Pierce 12t; David South 157br; Constantin Stanciu 40tl; Wayan Sulendra 131tr; Mulawardi Sutanto 44tl; Ariyani Tedjo 34tl, 35cl; travelib Indonesia 46bl; Yuliya Trukhan 141bl; Dray van Beeck 37c; Mykola Velychko 24cl; Nitish Waila 12–13b; Rob Walls 100bl; Christine Wehrmeier 27ca; Michel & Gabrielle Therin-Weise 154cra; Karin De Winter 163br; Jan Wlodarczyk 10ca, 154clb; Poelzer Wolfgang 138b.

AWL Images: Marco Bottigelli 18tl, 112–13; Michele Falzone 2–3, 69t.

Bridgeman Images: Christie's Images / Willem Gerard Hofker © DACS 2018 *Phantastic Bali, poster advertising the Bali Hotel, Indonesia* 56tl; Pictures from History 54bl, 55tr, 55cr, 99br.

Courtesy of Ashtari Lombok: 24br.

Depositphotos Inc: luckybusiness 10clb; tashka2000 48–9t.

Dreamstime.com: Amadeustx 124bl; Christophe Amerijckx 13t; John Anderson 162t; Arttikstockphotography 42clb; Kairi Aun 116clb; Kitchner Bain 95tr; Florian Blümm 153cb; Shariff Che\' Lah 125tl; Christophefaugere 175br; Tomas Ciernik 160b; Cmeili87 33c; Cocosbounty 102b, 165bc; Dvrcan 98–9t; Feathercollector 149cra; Aqnus Febriyant 74b; Oliver Förstner 123tr; Elizaveta Galitskaya 94–5b; Galjan 116b, 119t; Bradley Hay 157cl; Idmanjoe 118cl; Dmitry Islentyev 51ca; Joyfull 80–81t; Elena Krutikova 43b; Lakhesis 96t; Leoraduga 174–5t; Lev Levin 119bc; Edmund Lowe 35crb, 49br, 50–51t; Denis Moskvinov 4; Christian Nilsen 175tc; Jon Chica Parada 181t; Tomas Pavlasek 44–5b; Marek Poplawski 154–5; Tawatchai Prakobkit 166–7b; Anthony Prince 187tl; Ruengrit 30t; Oktobernardi Salam 23tr, 148; Softlightaa 19, 168–9; Somma695 68bl; Nikolai Sorokin 164clb; Hiroshi Tateishi 125tr; Telnyawka 159cr; Matthew Train 6–7; Venemama 126t; Andra Wayan 133tr; Weltreisendertj 123cr; Wonderful Nature 84tl; Tayfun Sertan Yaman 149crb.

Getty Images: AFP / Jewel Samad 59cr, / Sonny Tumbelaka 53tr, 59tr, / STR 59br; Bettmann 56clb; Raung Binaia 142–3b; Larry Burrows 58bc; Culture Club 54crb; Fadil Aziz / Alcibbum Photography 189t; Michele Falzone 18cb, 134, 144–5; John Florea 57tr; Isa Foltin 167tr; IN2 Focus Media 188b; Justin Ong 53br; Agung Parameswara 52cla; raditya 178–9t; James R.D. Scott 177tr; simonlong 58–9t, 117; Terence Spencer 58tl; Maria Swärd 186–7b; Andrew TB Tan 22–3ca; torstenvelden 120–11t; Maya Vidon-White 59clb; Alfian Widiantono 172cra, 182–3b.

iStockphoto.com: AlenaPaulus 176cra; asiafoto 131tl; Bicho_raro 88–9t; Valery Bocman 121crb; Em Campos 48–9b; CEphoto, Uwe Aranas 81br; ChanwitOhm 45tr; Csondy 10–11b; Andrey Danilovich 8–9; dietrichherlan 76t; dislentev 83t; DKart 17, 90–91; enviromantic 34b; ErmakovaElena 190–91; Goddard_Photography 131cla; ifew 32b; joakimbkk 32tl; johan10 57bc; jon11 46–7t; KellyOla 34cra; KitHamilton 149clb; LadyBird89 8cl; laughingmango 8clb; mahroch 28t; manjik 16, 62–3; master2 69cra, 72–3b; MelanieMaya 30clb; miralex 119bc, 128bl; Myslitel 33br; NicoElNino 11br; Nikada 97cra; PrinPrince 172bl; raung 8cla, 33tl; RibeirodosSantos 60–61, 78–9t; Iuliia Serova 66tr; Shrekton 13cr; steffie82 183tr; swissmediavision 38–9t; Aleh Varanishcha 30br.

Mowie's: 26–7ca.

Picfair.com: Theodora 53cl.

Rex by Shutterstock: EPA / Made Nagi 53cr.

Robert Harding Picture Library: G & M Therin-Weise 125cla, 154bc.

SuperStock: age fotostock / Carol Buchanan 95tl, / Jan Wlodarczyk 20cr, / Leonid Serebrennikov 12clb, / Manfred Gottschalk 51br; Axiom Photographic / Design Pics / Peter Langer 28crb; Cultura Limited 176–7b; imageBROKER / Moritz Wolf 52cra; Mauritius 149cl.

Ubud Writers & Readers Festival: Anggara Mahendra 52crb.

Front Flap:
123RF.com: Aleksandar Todorovic cb; **Alamy Stock Photo:** Dima Fadeev cra; Jon Arnold Images Ltd cla; **Getty Images:** James R.D. Scott bl; **iStockphoto.com:** DKart br; **SuperStock:** Cultura Limited tc.

Cover images:
Front and Spine: **AWL Images:** Michele Falzone.
Back: **Alamy Stock Photo:** Michele Falzone cla; **AWL Images:** Michele Falzone bc; **Dreamstime. com:** Denis Moskvinov c; Tawatchai Prakobkit tr.

For further information see: www.dkimages.com

Penguin Random House

Main Contributors Rachel Lovelock, Andy Barski, Albert Beaucourt, Bruce Carpenter, John Cooke, Jean Couteau, Diana Darling, Sarah Dougherty, Julia Goh, Lorca Lueras, Tim Stuart, Tony Tilford

Senior Editor Alison McGill

Senior Designer Laura O'Brien

Project Editor Rada Radojicic

Project Art Editors Ben Hinks, Sara-Louise Brown, Tom Forge, Ankita Sharma, Priyanka Thakur

Factchecker Ron Emmons

Editor Sands Publishing Solutions

Proofreader Kathryn Glendenning

Indexer Zoe Ross

Senior Picture Researcher Ellen Root

Picture Research Harriet Whitaker

Illustrators Anuar Bin Abdul Rahim, Denis Chai Kah Yune, Chang Huai-Yan, Choong Fook San, Koon Wai Leong, Lee Yoke Ling, Poo Lee Ming, Thomas Sui, Peggy Tan, Yeap Kok Chien

Cartographic Editor James Macdonald

Cartography Simonetta Giori, Zafar ul Islam Khan, Era-Maptech LTD

Jacket Designers Maxine Pedliham, Vinita Venugopal, Simon Thompson

Jacket Picture Research Susie Peachey

Senior DTP Designer Jason Little

DTP Designer Azeem Siddiqui

Senior Producer Stephanie McConnell

Managing Editor Rachel Fox

Art Director Maxine Pedliham

Publishing Director Georgina Dee

The information in this DK Eyewitness Travel Guide is checked regularly.
Every effort has been made to ensure that this book is as up-to-date as possible at the time of going to press. Some details, however, such as telephone numbers, opening hours, prices, gallery hanging arrangements and travel information, are liable to change. The publishers cannot accept responsibility for any consequences arising from the use of this book, nor for any material on third party websites, and cannot guarantee that any website address in this book will be a suitable source of travel information. We value the views and suggestions of our readers very highly. Please write to: Publisher, DK Eyewitness Travel Guides, Dorling Kindersley, 80 Strand, London, WC2R 0RL, UK, or email: travelguides@dk.com

First edition 2001

Published in Great Britain by Dorling Kindersley Limited, 80 Strand, London, WC2R 0RL

Published in the United States by DK Publishing, 1450 Broadway, 8th Floor, New York, NY 10018

Copyright © 2001, 2019 Dorling Kindersley Limited
A Penguin Random House Company
19 20 21 22 10 9 8 7 6 5 4 3 2 1

A CIP catalog record for this book is available from the British Library.

A catalog record for this book is available from the Library of Congress.

ISSN: 1542 1554
ISBN: 978 0 2413 6004 0

Printed and bound in Malaysia.

www.dk.com